A Bite of
Arkansas

A Bite of
Arkansas

A Cookbook of Natural State Delights

Kat Robinson

TONTI
PRESS

Published by Tonti Press
Little Rock, Arkansas
Copyright © 2020 by Kat Robinson. All rights reserved.

All photography by Kat Robinson

First published December 2020

Manufactured in the United States of America

ISBN: 978-1-952547-01-0

Library of Congress Control Number: 2020948388

Softcover release January 2021

ISBN: 978-1-952547-00-3

The author accepted no compensation for inclusion of any element in
this book. All photographs of food consist of edible, real food
cooked by the author or, in a few cases, her family,
not enhanced with photographic tricks, manipulation or fakery.

To all of us.

The trials of 2020 have affected us all.

Better days are ahead.

FOREWORD

Early evening, washing dishes, looking out the window over the blue glass bottles to my CR-V, which had for the most part just sat in that space for the past several weeks. The light was starting to stay later into dinnertimes, and outside I could hear something that had evaporated months ago - the sound of young folks in the street, talking, riding bikes, and... just being..

As I ran the washcloth inside a glass jar, I took a breath, and just concentrated on that sound. I couldn't make out the words, but I could feel the emotion behind them, the relief at seeing other people, even from across a street or several bike-lengths away. Maybe things would be okay.

The oven creaked behind me as it cooled. The remainder of a casserole sat on a burner, awaiting the black and clear takeout box I'd slide it into, to take its place on a shelf in the fridge. My shirt was wet, my feet were bare, the hum of the television two rooms away a bare static on the night.

My daughter sat at the dining room table, conversing with her fellow Girl Scouts on yet another Zoom, attempting some sort of normality. But this wasn't normal.

Three months earlier, we'd have been in our own house, if I was even home. If it was a home day, we'd be coming in the door from the long drive home from school, the one that could take an hour depending on traffic but, if I were to have gone this particular day, might have been ten minutes, tops. Grav would have been coming in from the Innovation Hub, and would be asking what we wanted for dinner as Hunter would take her bag to her room, then bring in her lunchbox and fill it with the convenient foods for the next day, tucking it into the bottom of the refrigerator. I'd be picking up the computer again after sitting down in my recliner, ready to dive back into the story or the podcast or the video I was producing at the time. Later dinner would appear at my elbow, and then Hunter would be singing me our good night song, and eventually I'd wake at 2 a.m. when the computer clicked off, wander back to my room and sleep a few more hours before getting up the next day.

Or, often as not, I'd be wherever I had landed, done with my shooting at the end of the day, just checked into a hotel or an AirBNB, just done photographing it for later, snacking on leftovers from whatever food shoot i had while editing together a story or setting up a book order or corresponding with someone about a public appearance. Sometimes I'd go out once more to capture another restaurant or an evening event, only to return and prep for the next day and sit at my computer until I fell asleep.

But that was weeks, or years, ago, back when life kept coming every single day, when the hustle never stopped. I was lucky. I could travel and write and shoot and diversify and put 300 miles on my tires every day, as long as I had the stamina.

That wasn't now. It was late May, and I hadn't put gas in my CRV since March 11th.

There was a dishwasher right next to me, but the hot water felt real, and the surfaces of every dish smoothed under my hands as particulates came off. This little kitchen I could keep clean, washing dishes every evening and wandering in each morning to make chai and wiping down all the tile with a cleaner that smelled like grapefruit.

I had lights to haul into the kitchen later in the evening, the big desk and floor lamps I was re-purposing from the den to illuminate the white kitchen enough to shoot my video segments for the upcoming special. They were heavy, their light melting me within minutes each time I set the shot. It hurt, all the stretching to get the lights and cameras in place, clamping an old cell phone up as a makeshift monitor, reaching for heavy pots and skillets and organizing my mise en place for each dish. It was important to get everything shot for the video segments that would air both on TV and on YouTube, a valiant weird no-contact effort at a cooking show by a woman who had spent way too much time in other kitchens and dining rooms these past 13 years.

For now, though, there were just the memories, decades flowing back into my head, alongside the pain of grease pops while frying and the steam from boiling water and the tiny abrasions on my thumbs from remembering how to slice again, and the dishwater.

This was my life the first few months of the pandemic. They were to have been the beginning of my new normal, putting together a travel podcast in-between public appearances, publishing books and occasionally updating my website with another longform story. I'd been doing a lot of food photographer gigs in the winter ahead of the keynotes that would come in April, May and June. I had two books in the collection stage - one on cheese dip, one on catfish - that would be my paired books for the year. My schedule was airtight. I knew where I was going, what I was going to do. I had a thickly packed shoot schedule ready to go to share our great state agritourism sites. My career was thriving.

And then it was gone. Over one week, I lost all but one of 22 set appearances, which meant honorariums that would not be paid and book sales that wouldn't be made. That last one held out until May before being canceled. The Arkansas Pie Festival, which was partly inspired by my books and show, was quietly put away for another year.

I scrambled to get Grav set up with enough equipment to keep his business going. And then at some point I retreated across Markham to another house, my mom's roost - going over one day for a Zoom, a second day for Easter dinner and then not going home. My daughter took over the dining room table with her makeshift school and all her art supplies. Grav brought my spice bag and my camera bag and more than 400 of my collected church cookbooks, and left me alone, only to apparate at dinner each night.

My mom brought food. While we were hunkering down, she was still out working as a hospice nurse, out overnight. She's how I found out the 24 hour grocery stores were a thing of the past, and who hauled in random supplies I'd use to conjure edible memories and experiments. Grav would deliver the pick-up orders from Kroger, the crapshoots in the beginning that would determine what I'd make each day. We'd stock the pantry at both houses, not knowing how long we'd be holding out.

And every day, I'd head to the kitchen when I first woke up, making my chai and filling the numbness of the situation with what I could bring to the table. My daughter, never before experiencing the wonder of sausage balls, hammered breakfast steak, sugared rice or beer muffins, would silently brag to other students on the Zooms by showing off her plate and her cup of well creamed coffee, never progressing much beyond a selection of onesies between showers, while her teachers tried hard to compensate for the evaporation of an in-person sixth grade year.

After a breakfast made, I'd pick up seven or eight cookbooks, using my mom's pen cups contents to mark spaces, recording on my phone ingredients to acquire. After a lunch usually comprised of leftovers from the previous night, I'd start prepping ingredients. After Hunter's schooling had ended for the day, the kitchen would come alive with the clatter and sound of whisks making roux and timers going off, notes hurriedly spoken into my phone while I'd dart back and forth between two or three recipes. The pile of cookbooks would become unmanageable, spilling onto the lower section of the bar, displacing the dry goods I wanted close at hand.

When, an hour or two or three had passed and the meal had come together, I'd pull out a light ring and plug it in to compensate for the darkness that consumed most of the house. I'd take photos on my phone, lacking the will to go to the next room and get my Canon Rebel with the good lens, just documenting what little I had done. And when everyone was fed, I'd pack the leftovers - a plate for Mom, a plastic container for Grav to take back across Markham with him for snacking later, the rest for Hunter and I to dig through for lunch the next day. I'd retreat back to the computer to enter my notes, and then I would make myself get out of the chair at 11 p.m. and go back to the guest bedroom and sleep as best I could on the single bed, to awaken at six in the morning and start again.

***

"As best I could" was the most succinct definition of what I was doing. The world was closing down, and then it was quiet, shocked into a new format of existence. I'd sometimes lay in that corner room, wondering why I couldn't hear the city. The wind would sometimes sweep up, or a cat would be heard long in the distance. The houses all around us were occupied but we all seemed to keep to our stunned silence.

Ghosts would come. No, not the essence of spirits hovering over my bed, but of awakened memories from decades ago, memories of high school and before, and after, and of dishes that I had failed to fully appreciate when I was younger. I would dream of how the light filtered down in a space, and wake tasting those dreams. In-between, I dreamed of driving, the miles clacking away under my tires, vistas of the Ozarks spread out in the distance or of Delta sunrises, or of winding Timberland roads through canyons of pines. I grieved.

My sense of purpose was diluted. I recorded segments of the TV show, talking to myself through the camera, feeling like a dolt. I typed my redactions and corrections off every recipe I tried. I sometimes doomscrolled Facebook and Twitter and felt so guilty, seeing my restaurant friends doing everything they could to keep going and not knowing how I could help.

I also saw a thousand new bakers created, as people learned sourdough and coveted yeast. Scenes were crafted in the narratives of so many I knew and loved, recipes shared, tables filled with food worthy of a Thanksgiving banquet, shared between two or three, the rest packed up for meals that would sustain for weeks, sometimes even traded for the culinary creations of others. I asked for many of

11

those recipes, and months later I'd publish a collection, *43 Tables: An Internet Community Cooks During Quarantine*. It wasn't about earnings I might generate, but the idea of doing something, anything, that might have meaning through this. Also, for smiles. We all needed smiles.

May passed into June, and with new guidelines released I'd don my mask, hood, hat and gloves and head to a few farmers markets and farms for the fresh produce I craved. The TV show, *Home Cooking with Kat and Friends*, debuted. The ache in my shoulder that nagged at me every time I cooked blossomed to a point where those nights laying in the single bed became excruciating sojourns that ate at me. I'd find out in July it was bad, and I packed up my spices and went home and cleaned house as best I could until I had surgery to correct my shoulder and lost the next three months.

It's now October. There's an agitation in the air with the election, less than two weeks away at this point. I've stopped washing the dishes by hand, now that I'm back in my home and the dishwasher works, though its installation sadly lead to a leak that destroyed much of my kitchen floor. I don't know where the funds will come from to put something down over the new subfloor that Grav and Leif installed, but I do know how the patio rug I found feels on my feet and where my spices have migrated to around the galley. There's a bite of cold in the air that comes from nights without the central heat and air, usually mitigated by my cat sleeping on my knees on the other side of the computer, which sits on my lapdesk at my waist while I snooze, propped up since I can't roll over until my shoulder heals a bit more.

I haven't slept outside of Little Rock since early March, but when I do sleep, I feel a peace. Memories that came to crest in my imagination while I was standing at the sink have now come to the table, been shot and shared and now memorialized in the pages of a book I never thought I'd be writing, a combination of those unearthed flavors and a memoir that may only matter to me.

Because, you see, I was brought up Arkansas. I had the chances to leave - for college, for work, for love - and I stayed. I am planted in this soil. These flavors I share are just as much about what shaped me as what I eat, and what others eat. When it was conceived, it was supposed to just be a cookbook. It's something... different? More? I can't quite say.

It is personal. And I think , after all this time in my own head, unable to escape on the road to new destinations and the stories of others, I can properly share it.

Eat well.

Kat Robinson   October 24, 2020

All of these recipes were made and photographed in 2020 on a Samsung S8 photos. Each and every dish was made by hand and is photographed "as is" with no photographic trickery or modeling. Every dish was edible and consumed, most with a great deal of glee and enjoyment.

The stories within are the best recollection I have. Time may have bent some experiences in memory, but the essence of each story is there.

These are my mom's dishes. Her collection is wonderful and diverse. It was a joy to use them for this book.

Upon Awakening

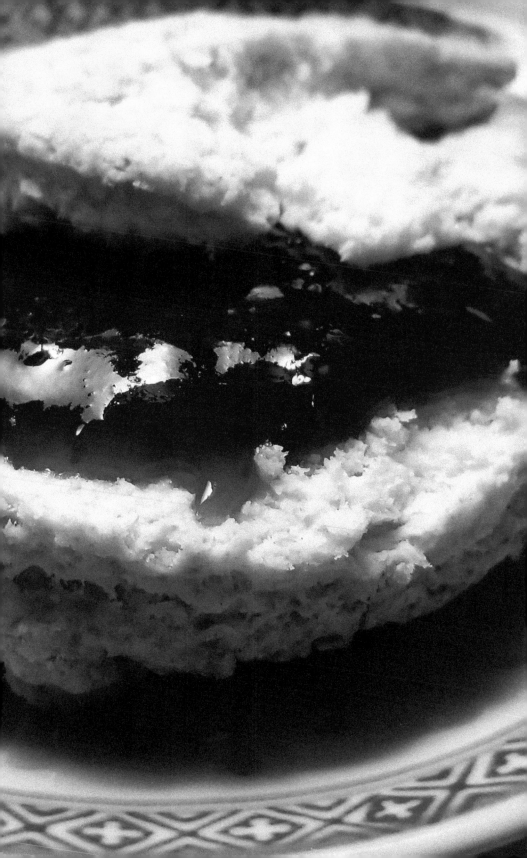

I used to wake up some Saturday mornings, to a banging barrage on the kitchen counter. When I'd hear that noise, I'd roll out of bed, head to the hall bath, perform my ablutions, and wander into the kitchen.

The temperature between the always cold formal dining room and the laden air of the kitchen came with the scent of coffee, the pop of an inch of Crisco in a cast iron pan and the continued beating of venison or beef under Grandma Bear's big wooden spiked mallet. She'd pound them until they were half an inch thick, then dredge them in flour, salt and pepper and drop them into the sizzling grease, to be followed by eggs she'd expertly cracked on the side of the skillet, their edges curling up brown so quick once they'd hit the surface, floating just high enough for the spatula to get under them for a flip. In-between, the door to the oven would squeal when she'd pull it open, grabbing a pan of biscuits from the rack with a dish towel.

I'd go sit at my place in the corner between the kitchen bar and the family table, always on the harder to reach long side of the table, next to Grandpa Bear on the corner. He would already be up with his coffee and saucer. He'd pour milk into the coffee, then tilt the cup just a little and fill the saucer. His wrinkled hand would tremble as he lifted the saucer to sit atop his lower lip from the old brown melamine dish. He'd carefully put it down again with his one arm and tilt the coffee in once more.

Grandma Bear would always have butter out on the table, and syrup in a push-slide dispenser, the type you'd press with your thumb that'd slide open the top. There would be one or two open jars of jam, a plate of biscuits and another topped with paper towels dappled brown with grease spots, laden with the meat of the day, bacon or sausage or those hand hammered country fried breakfast steaks. The venison ones would be chewier than

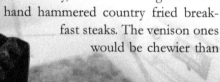

17

the beef ones, but they were always made better with gravy Grandma would have in an old Pyrex glass bowl, green on the outside, white within. I'd drag the little sausage patties she'd make through syrup and eat them like that, saving my biscuits for the jam and butter. The eggs would get a little syrup in them, too, the yolk running into the edges of my plate when I'd break in with my fork between the dousing of black pepper on top.

There was sometimes milk and sometimes something akin to orange juice, maybe even Tang, but my drink of choice was a melamine cup filled with milk and sugar and a splash of coffee, and a glass of the sweet water that came from the well.

Grandma Bear indulged us sometimes. One thing I loved was the sugared rice. I cannot recall if I asked for it the first time or if it appeared before me, perhaps on one of those very early mornings before fishing or deer hunting. I just remember this bowl of rice, sticky from the pan in which it had been reheated, with a teaspoon of sugar and an ample spoonful of margarine on top. Other times that rice would end up with gravy on it - but that was far more likely to happen at dinner, gravy on rice.

I don't ever remember her making waffles, though pancakes came sometimes. Cantaloupe was another visitor to the table each summer, syrupy sweet in long, curved wedges. Strawberries would be there in season, as would apples, fried lightly, in the fall.

I do remember breakfast was done for Grampa Bear when he finished his coffee and reached in his overalls pocket for his flask-shaped can of Prince Albert, and the scent of the tobacco while he used his finger and thumb to liberate a sheet from the rolling papers in that matchbook shaped package, spreading it flat with thumb and ring finger, then carefully tipping in a row. He'd roll it on the table, finger to palm, then crunch one end a bit. It'd end up pinched between his fingers as he would get up, pushing the chair back with the back of the legs, hitting the edge of the windowsill. He'd have the cigarette in his one hand while fishing out his lighter with his thumb, somehow managing to flip the tip of the Zippo just right and catching the crimped in with the flame, before snapping the top shut and letting it slide back down in his pocket. By the time he lit his cigarette, Grandma Bear was already clearing the table.

If the pounding of the mallet on meat didn't get you up, or if you missed your alarm, you were just out of luck and didn't get that table service. Usually, though, there were biscuits left over, kept in a pan on the back of the stove, for those who came early or late, to pick at until lunch came about.

BEEF or VENISON BREAKFAST STEAKS

1 pound beef or venison cutlet, preferably chuck or roast,
  sliced into 6-8 pieces against the grain
1 perforating mallet
1 cup all purpose flour
1 teaspoon black pepper
1/2 teaspoon salt
Crisco or oil for frying (lard or bacon drippings also acceptable)

Heat grease to popping, medium-high. Sift together flour, pepper and salt.

On a cutting board, pound beef or venison to a thickness of no more
than 3/4 of an inch in thickness.

Dredge meat in flour mixture, then lay into the grease and cook 2-3
minutes each side. Remove to paper towels to drain. Serve hot.

19

Every cook I knew growing up had a can or pan of grease on the back of the stove. Both of my grandparents, all of my aunts, my mom, even eventually me, we all had some form of grease collection gathered into a receptacle that was within easy reach of our spoons or spatulas when we cooked.

The grease that would collect in these containers was meant to lubricate the pan, to get started what would cook within. It was collected from what was rendered in the cooking of bacon and sausage at breakfast, ground beef for casseroles or burgers for dinner, just drained off into the can at the end of the meal before the cast iron skillet was wiped down and placed at the back of the stove for whatever came next. In the morning, a scoop at the end of a spatula would come out, to be smacked from the end of the utensil right into the pan, the sound of the conk of the metal implement's edge and its subsequent sizzle in the hot pan a call to get your shower over and clothes on because breakfast would be there and ready to go as soon as you got dressed.

I didn't translate that into the goodness it brought to dishes until I was an adult, attempting to make cornbread the first few times. I didn't understand why I didn't have the caramelized, crispy edges on the edge of my slices. It didn't come with just a little butter smeared on the side, and the flavor didn't come through with Crisco.

Nor did I understand the value of its role in the gravy process, when time was tight and especially when meat was not on the menu. But I would come to know its power.

My brother didn't know that value either, particularly when he was a toddler. One Sunday morning in my high school years, after a day of band activities that had gone into the late hours the day before, I had hoped to sleep in. I was awakened to heavy, fast footfalls, a squeal, and then the fire alarm had gone off. Zack, exploring the house as we drowsed, wandered his three year old self into the kitchen and grabbed at things. We had childproofed the drawers and cabinet doors to little avail; he quickly ripped through the plastic door tongs with almost glee (an act my daughter would replicate some 23 years later) but he had no access to sharp objects nor the ability to lift heavy pots; the chemicals for cleaning were secured out of his reach.

Somehow, we never considered the stove an issue. Yet Zack managed to get the stove to spark and flame, igniting the pan of grease and starting a contained blaze that woke his father and caused the ruckus, as his dad grabbed the handle of the flaming skillet, ran to the back door and hurled the still-flaming pan into the backyard.

This one incident made me a cautious adult. My grease always came out of the pan at the end, to be held in a bowl or jar away from potential flames. When I took on healthier cooking later on, I utilized the Can The Grease program our water and sewer folks offered, allowing the grease to cool in a plastic lined tin before disposing of it in my backyard, particularly at the back corner. I still sometimes keep grease, but only when gravy is on my horizon.

PAN FRIED POTATOES

1 pound potatoes, skin on, any type (Yukon Gold or Redskin work best)
1 onion
1 Tablespoon butter or back-of-the-stove grease from breakfast meat
Salt and pepper to taste

Cut potatoes into 1" cubes (perfection not necessary). Dice onions.

In a heavy skillet, melt butter or grease over medium heat. Add potatoes and onions. Place on back burner over medium heat while the rest of breakfast is prepared. Stir potatoes and onions occasionally to prevent burning. Cook until potatoes are soft and onions are translucent.

Quicker version: Use baked potatoes prepared in advance (great f extras left over from the night before).

CRUMBLY SCONE BISCUITS

2 cups all-purpose flour
1 Tablespoon baking powder
2 teaspoons sugar
1/2 teaspoon salt

1/2 teaspoon cream of tartar
1/2 cup salted butter, chilled
2/3 cup milk

Preheat oven to 425 degrees.

Sift together flour, baking powder, sugar, cream of tartar and salt. Use a pastry blender or your fingers to cut the butter into the dry ingredients until it forms coarse crumbs. Add in milk and stir gently with a fork until the dough comes together.

Lightly flour the counter. Knead the dough on the counter until it smoothes out. Roll it 1/2 an inch thick, then cut it with a biscuit cutter or a clean 15 ounce vegetable can. Place rounds on baking sheet. Form dough back into ball, roll out to 1/2 inch again and cut what you can again. The last few will be crumbly - but that's OK. They'll eat, too.

Bake for 10-12 minutes, or until risen and a golden brown. Serve with gravy, honey, butter, jam, jelly or whatever you like.

DROP BISCUITS

2 cups all-purpose flour
1 Tablespoon baking powder
1 teaspoon kosher salt
1 stick salted butter, chilled

1 cup buttermilk
or 3/4 cup milk and 1/2
teaspoon lemon juice,
whisked together

Preheat oven to 450 degrees.

Whisk together flour, baking powder, and salt together. Cut cold butter into dry ingredients with a pastry cutter or fork until the consistency of coarse meal.

Add buttermilk or milk and lemon juice mixture in splashes until just combined, until the batter is no longer dry. Do not overmix.

With a large spoon (serving spoon), scoop and slightly roll mounds of biscuit. Drop them onto lightly oiled baking sheet or into cast iron skillet. Bake at 450 degrees for 18 to 22 minutes or until golden brown.

Mom would get me up shortly after six each morning, when I was still in my single digits.. She'd have the radio on while we shared the small bathroom, curling her hair and spritzing it with Final Net while Craig O'Neill would summon Sherman Bonner down from the roof to chat and tell the weather on KKYK. Most mornings I made it into the bathroom when the old, mystic music was playing announcing the horoscopes. Mom and I have birthdays a week and a half apart, and would try to turn on the radio in time to listen to what was up for Libras that day.

Breakfasts were quick affairs, often boiled eggs that had been set to cook right before Mom went to do her hair, sometimes boiled dry if we'd taken too long. Sometimes she'd fry an egg for a white bread sandwich with Miracle Whip. She would sometimes make up grits with cheese and bacon bits.

And on the luckiest days, particularly in winter, she'd heat the kitchen with the oven and slide a couple of slices of bread in to make cinnamon toast. That was the best.

I knew nothing of Cream of Wheat until I was in my late teens but I do remember oatmeal with brown sugar, and sometimes biscuits with butter and sorghum molasses. I'd inhale my breakfast and then we'd head out in time for her to drop me off at La Petite Academy before heading to the early shift at St. Vincent's Infirmary.

CINNAMON TOAST

4 pieces white or wheat bread   1 Tablespoon ground cinnamon
2 Tablespoons butter, softened   1 Tablespoon sugar

Combine cinnamon and sugar. Butter bread. Shake cinnamon and sugar evenly over slices. Place under a broiler or in a toaster oven and toast until sugar caramelizes. Serve hot, preferably with chocolate milk or hot cocoa.

GRITS FROM SCRATCH

Ratio:

4 cups water   1 cup grits
1 teaspoon salt   2 Tablespoons butter

Bring salt and water to a boil. Pour in grits, stir and cover, reducing heat to low. stirring occasionally, cooking for ten minutes. Remove from heat. Stir in salt and pepper to taste. Add in cheese, meat, gravy, or whatever you want.

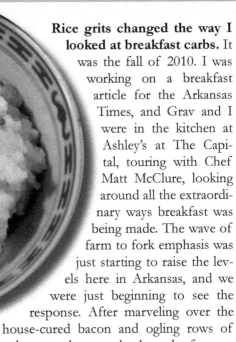

Rice grits changed the way I looked at breakfast carbs. It was the fall of 2010. I was working on a breakfast article for the Arkansas Times, and Grav and I were in the kitchen at Ashley's at The Capital, touring with Chef Matt McClure, looking around all the extraordinary ways breakfast was being made. The wave of farm to fork emphasis was just starting to raise the levels here in Arkansas, and we were just beginning to see the response. After marveling over the house-cured bacon and ogling rows of fresh quail eggs, Grav and I sat down to photograph a brunch of morning delights, which included a steaming bowl of cheesy, creamy, perfect grits made from house-processed Arkansas-grown rice. I was hooked.

Today, Ralston Farms of our marvelous Arkansas River Valley makes golden rice grits, which means they're just a cabinet door away from any breakfast I may make. They have earned their places as the base for winter bowls of grits topped with eggs and hot sausage and as a creamy sidecar for breakfast sandwich mornings.

HOW TO PREPARE RICE GRITS

2 1/2 cups water
3/4 cup rice grits
1/4 teaspoon salt

Bring water and salt to a boil. Add rice grits and stir.

Cover; set heat to low and simmer undisturbed 7-8 minutes.

Remove from heat and allow to sit 10 minutes before serving.

I like oatmeal. I'm not a fan of Cream of Wheat, but if I really want a hot breakfast cereal on a cold morning, **I adore sugared rice**. It reminds me of childhood.

In my twenties, I mentioned sugared rice to friends who had come into my circle during college and in the workplace. I discovered that it wasn't really a thing for most people - but for those who had eaten the breakfast delight before, it was always someone from Arkansas. Chef friends later confirmed this for me when I started asking about it during stories I was on. It was like a neat little Arkansas secret - this dish made from a staple our state produced more of than all other states, together. That's no joke - more rice is produced in Arkansas than all other American states, mostly in the Mississippi River Alluvial Plain but some in our Arkansas River Valley as well.

SUGARED RICE

2 cups water   2 Tablespoon butter
Pinch of salt   1 Tablespoon sugar
1 cup long grain rice   Dash of heavy cream (optional)

Bring water and salt to a boil. Add rice, cover and cut heat. Allow to sit 15 minutes.

Uncover, stir in butter and sugar (and cream if you'd like). Or, dollop into bowls and allow eaters to add their own butter and sugar as they wish.

CREAM GRAVY FROM SCRATCH
(or, how to make a roux for gravy)

1/2 cup butter (1 stick)	1/4 teaspoon salt
1/2 cup flour	1/4 teaspoon pepper
~ 1 cup milk	

Over medium high heat, melt butter until it begins to lightly brown. Add in flour and immediately begin to whisk together. Continue to whisk over medium-high heat until flour begins to brown. Allow flour to brown to your desired toastiness (anywhere from tan to chocolate). While continuing to whisk, pour in milk 1/4 cup at a time, until gravy reaches desired consistency. Remove from heat, continuing to whisk for two more minutes. Salt and pepper to taste.

Variations:

Sausage or bacon gravy: Fry sausage or bacon as desired, reserving grease. Add 1/2 grease back to pan. Omit butter. Continue as directed. Crumble sausage or bacon into gravy before serving.

Chicken cream gravy: Replace butter with rendered chicken fat. Replace half of the milk with chicken broth. Add poultry seasoning to taste.

THE TEN TYPES OF ARKANSAS GRAVY

Cream gravy (also referred to as milk gravy): Made with butter instead of drippings to create a roux, filled out with milk or cream to create a thick, rich meatless gravy. See facing page.

Sausage gravy (also called Sawmill gravy): Similar to cream gravy, but made with sausage grease for the roux and filled with chunks of crumbled sausage. See facing page.

Ham gravy: A cream gravy made with ham drippings, usually served over the same ham atop biscuits.

Brown gravy: A thin gravy made on a butter-and-roux base with beef broth, sometimes with added garlic.

Mushroom gravy: Similar to brown gravy, this cream-less gravy begins with a mushroom and butter or oil amalgamation, on which a roux is created. Beef broth is sometimes added.

Giblet gravy: A broth created with simmered turkey (or chicken) parts and mirepoix, thickened with cornstarch and often with hardboiled egg added.

Red gravy: Also referred to as "Sunday gravy," this is a tomato-based sauce sometimes thickened with a roux or with cream added.

Red-eye gravy: A viscous eye-opening gravy made from ham drippings and coffee.

Chicken cream gravy: Made from a thick roux from chicken fat, thickened with first flour and then milk or cream and chicken broth often peppered, sometimes enhanced with shredded chicken.

Chocolate gravy: An Arkansas specialty, this sweet gravy is made from butter, flour, cocoa powder and sugar to create a rich pour-over. See next page.

I never once encountered chocolate gravy until I was an adult. My family is from southwest Arkansas, and it just wasn't a thing while I was growing up. I suspect there are people in Arkansas who grew up on chocolate gravy who would have found sugared rice preposterous, so tit for tat.

Chocolate gravy in and of itself is believed to have its origins in Spain, of all places. Its American origins date back to Appalachian Kentucky, but here in Arkansas, it took hold in both the far-tucked places in the Ozarks and out in the Delta as well. It came about with the spread of alkaline or Dutch process cocoa - which is ground cocoa that's had alkaline agents added to it to fix the color, remove much of the cocoa butter and make the taste milder and less bitter. The process dates back to 1828, but its spread in America comes after the Civil War. No one knows who first decided to make a roux with flour, sugar and cocoa powder, but the resulting creation is certainly an Arkansas breakfast treat that merits attention.

I will note, after a prominent national magazine named chocolate gravy as Arkansas's unique food to celebrate, more restaurants made an attempt to put it on their menu. Some, however, misinterpreted the message and have, I kid you not, put chocolate pudding heated in a skillet up as chocolate gravy. This, in my opinion, is not good eats.

My daughter turned her nose up at the idea of chocolate gravy for years, until I whipped up this recipe. She ended up absconding with the remainder of the gravy from the batch, trying it out on everything from biscuits to Triscuits throughout the day.

CHOCOLATE GRAVY

3 Tablespoons butter
6 Tablespoons sugar
2 Tablespoons all-purpose flour
3 Tablespoons cocoa
2 cups milk

Heat butter in a skillet over low heat. Mix in sugar, flour, and cocoa.

Slowly pour one cup of milk into the skillet and whisk well to remove lumps.

Whisk in remaining milk, stirring constantly, until mixture is thick, being careful not to scorch.

Serve hot over biscuits.

31

I started making French toast for breakfast in my teen years. Mom gave me pretty much free reign of the kitchen and I had a collection of *Reader's Digest* that heralded back as far as the early 1960s, so I'd encountered quite a few recipes to sample. French toast was an excellent breakfast choice - it was easy to make, easy to eat and always a hit. I'd later go on to make egg-in-a-basket - essentially French toast with a runny yolk egg in the middle - that was well received by both my brother and later my husband.. The recipes are similar.

After spending time every New Orleans vacation at the New Orleans School of Cooking and encountering their excellent bread pudding recipe again and again, I was struck with the realization - French toast and bread pudding were essentially the same creation, just cooked differently. This opened my eyes. I soon started French toasting all sorts of bread, adding different items to the basket of my egg-in-a-basket, like chives and Cheddar cheese and pastrami and dill and whatever I felt like tackling.

Grav brought a new idea to the mix. I've been a frequent visitor to Julie's Bakeshoppe in Conway over time, and I have delighted in their day old honey buns and cinnamon rolls. Grav decided one day to split a cinnamon roll, French toast it, and serve it up crisp - no need for syrup or sweetener. A legend was created.

Not everyone can make it to Julie's for day-olds, but if you happen to have leftover doughnuts, you're in luck. This is an excellent way to re-purpose them. And if you have a LOT of leftover doughnuts, flip over the next page for my recipe for doughnut bread pudding.

FRENCH TOAST

8 slices desired bread
2 eggs
1/2 cup milk (more if bread is dry)

1 teaspoon butter, divided in half
1/2 teaspoon cinnamon (optional)
1 teaspoon sugar (optional)

Beat together egg, milk, sugar and cinnamon. Bring skillet to medium high heat. Melt butter in skillet. Dip both sides of each slice of bread in egg mixture, then lay it in the pan on the hot butter. Repeat with three more slices. Allow to fry 3 minutes, then flip and check for browning. Fry an additional three minutes. Flip to ensure browning on other side, then remove to wire rack or paper towels. Repeat with remaining butter and bread. Serve with syrup or jam.

DOUGHNUT FRENCH TOAST

4 glazed doughnuts, sliced horizontally
2 eggs

1/2 to 1 cup milk
1 teaspoon butter, divided

Beat egg and milk together. Melt butter in skillet. Dip both sides of each slice of bread in egg mixture, then lay it in the pan on the hot butter. Repeat with three more slices. Allow to fry 3 minutes, then flip and check for browning. Fry an additional three minutes. Flip to ensure browning on other side, then remove to wire rack or paper towels. Serve as is, no syrup necessary.

DOUGHNUT BREAD PUDDING

1 dozen doughnuts (any sort)   1 cup milk
4 eggs   1 teaspoon cinnamon (optional)

Crumble or cut doughnuts into 1 inch pieces. Heat oven to 350 degrees. Spray a 9x13 or similarly sized pan with cooking spray. Set aside. Beat together eggs and milk (and cinnamon, if using). Fold in doughnut chunks. Spread into pan. Allow to sit five minutes, then bake 45-50 minutes at 350 degrees. Pudding is done when inserted knife comes out clean.

BASIC BREAKFAST BREAD PUDDING RECIPE

4 cups bread of any sort   2 cups milk
4 eggs   1/2 cup sugar (for sweet puddings)

Beat together eggs and milk. Add sugar if making a sweet pudding. Fold in bread. Spread in 9x13 or similar pan. Bake at 350 degrees for 45-50 minutes or until knife comes out clean.

Breakfast bread pudding: Omit sugar. Fold in 1 cup fully cooked sausage, bacon or ham and one cup cheese. Cook as directed.

Sausage breakfast bread pudding: Cut sugar to 1/2 teaspoon. Add 1 pound browned sausage and cook as directed. Make a roux with 1/2 cup of the sausage drippings and 1/2 cup flour. When the gravy is made, add 1/2 teaspoon black pepper and 1/4 teaspoon salt. Pour over pudding before serving.

Reuben bread pudding: Omit sugar and use rye bread. Fold in one cup shredded corned beef and one cup Swiss cheese. Top with Russian dressing and serve with sauerkraut.

Though quiche dates back to the 14th century, the publication of the book *Real Men Don't Eat Quiche* by author Bruce Feirstein in 1982 not only made a joke of the dish, it brought the brunch favorite to the forefront of hungry minds across the country. Soon, everyone was making quiche, and it's stayed popular. It's a popular breakfast served at many Society for Creative Anachronism events because of its ease of making and serving. It's also common at so many buffets and on menus across Arkansas, usually with some version of pork. Dave's Place in downtown Little Rock always has a quiche special lunch, of which I have partaken many, many times.

QUICHE

1 pie crust, blind baked
4 eggs
2 cups half and half or 1 cup heavy cream and 1 cup milk
2 cups add-ins (pre-cooked meat, cheese, spinach, cooked vegetables)
1/4 teaspoon each salt and pepper
Herbs and spices to taste

Beat together eggs and dairy. Gently mix in add-ins. Pour into pie shell and bake 45-50 minutes at 350 degrees. Remove and allow to cool for 20 minutes before serving. Can be served hot or cold; refrigerate if not served in 45 minutes. Can be prepared a day in advance. Refrigerate leftovers.

We used to beat our apple tree. It would be sometime between Halloween and Thanksgiving, when we were done fishing for the year. It's a weird memory, but I remember the entire life cycle of the fishing poles. We'd cut cane in the late fall and shellac each pole to set up under a carport in the eaves for the next spring, several poles for each person who would fish. In the spring, the poles came down and would be used as long as they were viable. Sometimes an end joint or two would snap off, and either you had a shorter fishing pole or a stick to see how deep the water was. When it got too cold to reasonably fish, or when our thoughts had turned to hunting instead, the poles served another function - knocking the apples out of the tree on the east side of my grandparents' lawn. Helping the apples down meant we got them instead of the deer; the younger of us would watch where they fell to scoop them up. You had to make sure you hadn't grabbed one that had struck the ground days earlier - those would be soft and muckish.

Apples went into pie filling and into apple butter to put back for use throughout the year. Some few were eaten then; others left to sit a bit and get ripe. The really ripe ones that didn't make it into the jar went into fried apples instead, something that went well with breakfast.

Three decades later, I'd plan to get to Fort Smith early in the day to meet my photographer before shoots on the western side of Arkansas. That winter of early 2011, Arkansas Blackapples were plentiful at the local CV in the area, and it was common to scoot in and dine on fried apples with Grav before the day's adventure.

APPLE BUTTER

4-6 pounds apples, any sort (a blend is nice)	2 cups water
1 teaspoon salt, halved	1 teaspoon cinnamon
1 teaspoon lemon juice	1/2 teaspoon nutmeg
	1 teaspoon ground ginger

Cut apples into quarters or smaller, removing core and stem.

Place lemon juice, water and half teaspoon salt in pot. Put apples in water and simmer until the apples are tender.

Press through a colander, reserving liquid. Put mashed apples and liquid back in pot. Use an immersion blender to puree into applesauce.

Add cinnamon, nutmeg, ginger and remaining 1/2 teaspoon salt. Reduce to 1/2 volume. To can, use pressure method.

Serve over biscuits or toast or as a glaze or garnish for ham.

37

FRIED APPLES

3-4 firm apples, according to taste
1 Tablespoon salted butter
1 Tablespoon brown sugar
  or local honey

1 teaspoon cinnamon
1/2 teaspoon vanilla
1/2 teaspoon nutmeg (optional)
1 teaspoon lemon juice (optional)

Quarter and slice apples so that no piece is thicker than 1/2 inch. In a hot skillet, melt and brown butter. Add apples. Pour over sugar or honey and cinnamon. Stir together until apples are coated. Let simmer 5 minutes or until apples begin to soften.

Serve as a side dish for breakfast, reserving resulting sweet molten butter to brush on biscuits or pour over ice cream later.

JELLY or JAM

I seek out jams and jellies and homemade condiments these days. There's something about the way a person creates and cans a product from their own garden or land that appeals to me. This is common for Grav, too, who makes the jams and jellies that fill our pantry. Pickles? That's my territory - as you'll see later on in this book.

10 cups fruit of choice:
Berries, Figs, Peaches, Apples, or
peppers, chopped

5 cups sugar
1/2 cup lemon juice
1 5.4 ounce jar pectin

If making jelly, place fruit in blender or use immersion blender to render fruit to the consistency of applesauce. If making jam, reserve half of fruit and blend the remainder.

Place fruit in pot and bring to simmer. Add sugar and lemon juice and mix well, returning to a simmer. Stir regularly to prevent sticking or burning. When jam becomes sticky, add pectin. Allow to reduce until the jam is sticky enough to cause the spatula you're stirring with to stick to a plate enough to begin to pick it up. Use a hot water bath for canning. Store open jars in the refrigerator until use; otherwise, properly sealed jars should last in the pantry for up to a year.

When the pandemic came in March 2020, my friends turned to baking. I turned to Bisquick. The all purpose baking mix had long been absent from my pantry, out of some desire to be an authentic home cook making everything from scratch. But the pre-prepared mixture guaranteed to make cooking easier took on a more prominent place for me and Hunter.

Self-isolating and with school online each morning, I found myself wanting to give my daughter as normal a routine as possible. So at seven each morning, I'd get up and make my chai and her milk coffee, poke my head in and wake her up, and make her breakfast.

That box of Bisquick in my mom's cabinet quickly became many things - tamale pie, quick biscuits, and these two favorites - beer muffins and sausage balls. They make an easy, warm breakfast perfect for concealing in your hand while you're sitting on Zoom waiting for lessons to. start.

BEER MUFFINS

4 cups Bisquick
1 - 12 ounce bottle of can of beer
1/3 cup sugar
1/2 cup cheese (optional)

Preheat oven to 350. Lightly grease muffin tins for 18 muffins. Mix all ingredients together. Spoon into tins. Bake for 25 minutes or until tops become golden.

SAUSAGE BALLS

1 pound breakfast sausage (pork, beef, or turkey)
3 cups Bisquick
1/2 cup sharp Cheddar cheese

Preheat oven to 350 degrees.

Mix all ingredients together until the Bisquick no longer piles at the bottom of the bowl. Form into golf ball sized portions. Arrange in a foil lined 13"x9" baking pan (metal or glass), then bake for 20 minutes. Allow to stand and cool 10 minutes before serving. Can be made in advance and reheated two at a time in a microwave for one minute.

41

Fishing was a completely different lifestyle, with a food culture unto itself, from the moment you woke up to load up to the moment you pulled back in the driveway after a trip out.

Yes, we had coolers when I was young, but usually the Styrofoam boxes held bait or the fish we'd bring back in. Things we'd eat to head out in the morning and to sustain us fell in a different set of categories.

Fried bologna was common. It came at the time from Breitweiser's in Benton, thick sliced. It'd be fried the morning of the trip, wrapped back in its wax paper sandwiched between two slices of white bread lightly toasted. For variety, a white bread sandwich of fried egg and Miracle Whip might have been substituted, something that could be picked up and eaten in the truck o the way to the river.

I didn't know it was because bologna was ridiculously cheap back then. I just knew it never came out of the frying pan round, and that if you were out of bait, a chunk on a hook might earn you a big bream or sunfish, which could then be cut on the boat and immediately rehung to catch the much larger channel cats on the bottom of the stream.

HOW TO FRY BOLOGNA

1 pound beef bologna, cut 1/4 to 3/8ths inch thick (about four slices)
Toast and eggs to go with

Heat a skillet very hot. Cut through the bologna on a radius from center to edge.

When water pops when flicked onto the skillet, quickly lay bologna slices onto the surface. Allow to sit in place two minutes, then gently push against the edge of the slice. If the slice begins to move, it's ready to flip. Turn over bologna slice with fork or tongs, then allow to cook two minutes more, maintaining heat. Bologna is ready to be removed from the skillet when it's browned. If you like your bologna well-seared, keep cooking it.

The cut will allow the bologna slice to continue to lay flat against the bottom of the skillet. Without the slice, it'll dome up and you won't get an even cook.

Drain on paper towels. Serve with fried eggs and toast or use slices to make a sandwich.

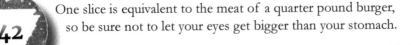

One slice is equivalent to the meat of a quarter pound burger, so be sure not to let your eyes get bigger than your stomach.

43

Almost everything I ever remember eating in a boat before I was an adult came from a box or a bag, not a cooler. There were occasionally things that would be what we would consider normal today - trail mix we made in Girl Scouts for canoeing on a lake, or Slim Jims or beef jerky for snacking on while dock fishing.

But early morning fishing trips had their own selection of items. Those almost always included the aforementioned bologna. More common were the chunks of Longhorn Colby or cheddar cheese, either obtained from Breitweiser's or from the counter at a bait shop. The foods that came from the bait shop were universal whatever part of the state I was in. Alongside the pickled eggs, pickled okra, pickled pigs feet and, well, pickles, would be a basket with plastic wrapped pieces of somewhat sweaty deep yellow cheddar cheese. The only proper way to enjoy this treat was at the end of a pocketknife, whether your own or someone else's, at the end of an outstretched hand.

Saltines were ubiquitous. A sleeve was always present. There always seemed to be Miracle Whip around, under the notion that it wasn't mayonnaise and therefore it would not go bad with heat. Strangely, I remember Miracle Whip being referred to as mayonnaise into adulthood as well, though the popular "creamy zip of Miracle Whip" commercials sought to educate folks otherwise.

And then, there were the twin cans that caused my soul to ache - little cans of Vienna sausages and potted meat product. The latter surfaced most often on the paternal side of my family, a protein easily available for the ridiculous price of a quarter a can back in the 1980s. The contents within would be smeared on a Miracle Whip topped cracker, gulped faster than a squeamish girl's first oyster encounter. I learned to not breathe through my nose when I went to swallow the cracker in a mouthful, two chews and a swallow, a poor man's fishing boat communion.

I've been told you can improve the flavor of Vienna sausages - which were just the same thing as potted meat product to me, but in a roll - by roasting it on a fire. Anyone who's ever tried to spear a Vienna sausage on a sharpened stick learns two things real quick: Vienna sausages aren't meant for spearing and roasting, and if you use the same stick for roasting marshmallows you're going to have a bad time.

Every once in a while, though, if I'm out on assignment and fishing is involved, I still seek out a hunk of sweaty yellow cheese from a bait shop counter, and enjoy the flavor that comes from the contrast, sometimes even with a lightly pickled egg.

45

Bites
In-Between

Sandwiches were the culinary currency of my elementary school days. I remember sandwiches shared and traded in the cafeteria at Geyer Springs Elementary - but I was a spectator in those occurrences. Usually I was handling a school lunch or fiddling with opening my Capri Sun without stabbing a hole in my hand. On days I did take my lunch, my white bread was intersected with a slice of coveted Pickle and Pimento Loaf.

Sandwiches at home were a different affair. They oscillated between two constants, pimento cheese and tuna fish sandwiches. The former was Miracle Whip, New York Sharp cheddar cheese and pimentos from those tiny jars. Forget the orange stuff in the tub at the supermarket - I wanted mine from the shreds produced by the four sided shredder, the job of shredding that usually fell to me, and the opportunity to snack on the ends that couldn't safely be pushed through.

Tuna fish - or, more succinctly, tuna salad, was something very particular to my mom's family. Later moments in my life were marked with the abject horror on the faces of my friends as I described the combination of Red Delicious apples and Chicken of the Sea, with the pickles and Miracle Whip and hard boiled egg. It wasn't weird to me then and I still sometimes find myself boiling eggs for a quart of salad to be consumed over the course of days, never having to share unless I'd made it at my mom's.

TUNA SALAD

2 cans chunk light tuna in spring water, drained

3 apples (1 cup) chopped apples (Gala or Red Delicious)

1 cup chopped dill pickle

6 hard boiled eggs (chopped)

1 cup Miracle Whip or mayonnaise

Fold all ingredients together. Serve or refrigerate promptly. Good in salads, in a scooped out tomato, or with crackers. Makes two pints.

PIMENTO CHEESE

2 cups shredded cheese (cheddar, Colby jack, Gouda recommended)
1/2 cup mayo or Miracle Whip
3-4 ounces diced pimento with reserved liquid

Combine. Keep refrigerated until ready to use..

My senior year at Arkansas Tech in Russellville, I shared a duplex behind Leonard's Hardware. From my living room, I could look down into the crowd that'd head through the double doors at Mrs. Meyer's across the street. The little neighborhood deli did hot plates and cold sandwiches. My selection was always a lunch plate that consisted of a peach half with cottage cheese and a tomato stuffed with tuna or chicken salad.

CHICKEN SALAD

3 cups cooked chicken breast, cubed
1/2 cup mayonnaise
1 Tablespoon apple cider vinegar
1 Tablespoon honey

1/4 teaspoon salt
1/3 cup chopped celery
1/3 cup white grapes, quartered
1/3 cup chopped pecans

Blend together mayo, vinegar, honey and salt. Toss with remaining ingredients. Refrigerate at least one hour before serving.

TURKEY CASHEW SALAD

2 cups shredded turkey
2 cups chopped apple (Opal, Gala, Honeycrisp or other sweet apple)
1/2 cup chopped cashews
1/2 cup chopped sweet pickles

3/4 cup Miracle Whip
1 teaspoon ground mustard
1 1/2 teaspoons sweet basil
1/2 teaspoon celery seed

Blend together Miracle Whip, ground mustard, basil and celery seed. Fold in other ingredients. Refrigerate an hour before serving.

One of my favorite albums is Paul Simon's *Graceland*. I wore out a cassette and played the tar out of a subsequent CD of the record over the decades. When my mom, brother and I made a trip to Memphis in the early aughts, Mom requested I play the title song as we headed to the home of Elvis for a tour. I started the song and sailed right past the exit on I-540, not realizing my error until we were nearly back to the river.

Elvis is tied to a particular combination of peanut butter and banana. He enjoyed the combination as a sandwich. To this day, the combination appears in everything from pancakes to burgers across our state - a land where The King dined over and over again. I've even joked that my third book, *Classic Eateries of the Arkansas Delta*, should have been called Elvis Eats Eastern Arkansas."

When I was pregnant with Hunter, I ate a peanut butter and banana sandwich just about every single day. Sadly, my daughter seems to be allergic to commercial peanut butter. More for me, I suppose.

PEANUT BUTTER AND BANANA SANDWICH

2 slices white bread   1 1/2 Tablespoon peanut butter
2/3 banana in 3/8 inch thick slices   1 Tablespoon honey or maple syrup

Blend together peanut butter and honey or syrup. Spread half on one side of each of the bread slices. Add banana slices and press both1 sides together. Serve with ice cold milk.

When speaking of sandwiches, pickles must be discussed. Hamburger dills with their ridgy appearance and flat notes were common with all sorts of burgers found at drive in restaurants and skating rink snack bars. Big dills in packets were often tucked into a cooler for enjoyment on camping trips. Tiny gherkins on toothpicks atop fancy sandwiches. But my favorites have to be bread and butter pickles, both sweet and full of flavor from coriander and mustard..

This is my recipe.

BREAD AND BUTTER PICKLES

2 quarts cucumbers
1/2 medium onion
1 green bell pepper
1 red or purple bell pepper (can substitute green)
1/2 cup coarse ground salt
Ice
2.5 cups vinegar
2.5 cups white sugar
1 Tablespoon ground turmeric
1 teaspoon mustard seed
1/2 teaspoon fennel seed
1/2 teaspoon dry ground mustard
\1/2 teaspoon celery flakes

Thinly slice cucumbers, onion and bell peppers. Toss in bowl with salt. Cover all with ice and allow to sit for three hours. Drain and lightly rinse vegetables.

Mix together vinegar, sugar, turmeric, ground mustard and celery flakes. In a small dry skillet, heat mustard and fennel seed until oil is released (you will hear seeds pop). Pour vinegar solution in and heat all together. Place vegetables in pot. Pour vinegar mixture over vegetables and simmer for one hour. Pack hot.

If you like them spicy, replace fennel seed with 1/2 teaspoon red pepper flakes and one crushed garlic clove.

If you like them really spicy, include all ingredients and add one whole small jalapeno to each pint jar before sealing. Very good with pastrami.

53

Mom worked very hard to keep us going when I was young. That meant a lot of time spent growing up with other kids. I remember staying with the Chambers and their sons at their house down the road from Eight Wheels, my favorite skating rink. Other times, I ran the streets around my abode, spending time with the neighborhood kids. I don't know if it was with the Dares or the Harringtons, but **someone introduced me to sloppy joes as a family dinner staple, and I dug it right away**.

Wherever it was, it was eaten with a fork because there's no way to make sloppy joes that won't disintegrate the bread (though toasting it does help some) and was usually served with chips on the side. In many ways, the dish is one of the most 80s things I can conjure, right along with Shake and Bake ("and I helped.")

While Manwich is still available to those who would want to conjure the saucy hamburger dish themselves, I have my go-to when the urge to dive in hits me. It's also an awesome pairing with potatoes, either on top or underneath with chunks of tomato in a makeshift shepherd's pie.

In college, I spent a ludicrous two weeks employed at the about-to-open Rally's location at Arkansas and 4th in Russellville in the summer of 1993. Fast food was never going to be my thing, and what I saw there pretty much put me off Rally's for life. One thing I did like, though, was the Rally Q - a sloppy joe sort of sandwich made in-house. And though I don't believe the Rally-Q is still a menu item, I do have the flavor of the sandwich pretty much down pat. Unlike the restaurant I worked at, the rejected hamburger, chicken fillets and ends of French fry bags aren't dumped into a constant bubbling pot of savory goo, but carefully measured into something resembling sanity.

CLEAN THE FRIDGE SLOPPY JOES

1 pound ground beef
1 pound ground chicken
1 yellow onion, diced
1/2 bell pepper, diced
1 1.2 cups ketchup
1 cup spaghetti sauce
1/3 cup water
1/3 cup yellow mustard
1 teaspoon Worcestershire sauce

1/2 teaspoon cayenne pepper
sauce (optional)
1 Tablespoon brown sugar
1 1/2 teaspoon garlic powder
1 teaspoon chili powder
1/2 teaspoon black pepper
1 cup breadcrumbs or cracker
crumbs, rendered fine

Brown together chicken, beef, onion and bell pepper. Combine all other ingredients except crumbs. Stir into meat mixture. Allow to simmer for 20 minutes. Incorporate bread crumbs completely and simmer five minutes more. Serve on buns or bread slices. Serves 12. Leftover burger sauce can be stored in an airtight container for 48 hours more, perfect for making a sandwich later.

RALLY-QS

1 pound ground beef
1/2 yellow onion, diced
1/2 bell pepper, diced
2/3 cup ketchup
1/3 cup water

1/3 cup yellow mustard
1 Tablespoon brown sugar
1 teaspoon garlic powder
1/2 teaspoon black pepper

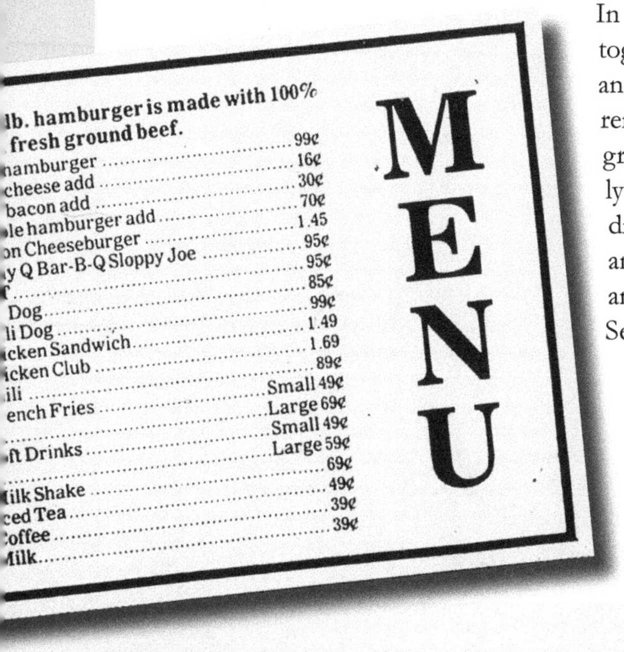

In a hot dry skillet, brown together ground beef, onion and bell pepper. Stir together remaining ingredients. When ground beef has completely browned in pan (do not drain), add ketchup mixture and stir. Reduce to simmer and let cook 20 minutes. Serve on buns or sliced bread.

In my single digits, there were two types of cheese and chip nights.
One would be my mom making nachos in her 13 x 9 Oster casserole dish
with the blue flower motif on the side. She'd carefully lay out a handful
of tortilla chips, top them with rat trap cheddar cheese (what was then
branded as New York Sharp), spread a handful of jalapenos and then
bake for twenty minutes. We'd share it, me picking off the jalapenos, while
watching TV or just sitting at the kitchen table. She often added a can of
chili with beans, lettuce, diced tomatoes, and sour cream.

The other type would come when the Velveeta would be pulled out and
cubed, dropped into the Crock Pot with a can of Ro*Tel and left to heat
while party food was made - crab meat mold, ham ball, shrimp boiled
in beer. Mom would send me across the street to the Harringtons, and
Mr. Harrington would climb in the back of his Frito Lay truck and pull
out bags of tortilla chips and Doritos, which we'd exchange for a dollar
apiece. Mom's friends would come over and maybe some kids my age and
I'd have a Sprite and a jar of maraschino cherries for my very own Shirley
Temples. The Velveeta and Ro*Tel cheese dip would be ladled onto paper
plates with chips and what was left at the end of the night was a skin of
the cheese product at the bottom of the turned-off Crock-Pot, which I
could pull out in stringy chunks and eat by themselves.

There were other cheese dip times, like driving out to Prothro Junction
and going through the drive-thru, once it opened, at Mexico Chiquito.
We'd get a cheese dip, a bag of chips, and an order of sopaipillas. If there
were any other dishes ordered, I knew not of them, because all I wanted
were chips covered in dip and sopaipillas filled with honey. Taco Kid was
closer, but the dip was flatter, with fewer spices. And while like many kids
I relished the chance to spend an afternoon at Casa Bonita, it was for the
punch and the Treasure Room and not for the dip there, which had a
plain sigh to it and which, when it was sold and became Casa Viva, turned
to something that quite approximated Campbell's Cheddar Cheese Soup.

Both dishes cemented a love of soupy cheese that has remained a thread
in my life. As a high school student, there were plenty of pass-around
paper trays of what Parkview called nachos that were just canned cheese
poured over chips, either at lunch or at a football game. When I got to
Tech, there was the pure joy of the cheapest Mexican I've ever known,
Taco Villa on 4th Street, where the only real difference between the taco
salad and nachos was the order in which the lettuce, chips, cheese, and the
rest went into the box. My first week in Jonesboro saw me at Taco Rio
in a back corner, watching people and feeling strange and alone. At Casa
Manana, when I'd return home to Little Rock, the dip was white and
would tack to the roof of my mouth. And when the 21st century
arrived and we'd gather in my home to celebrate, out again would

come the Velveeta. I stopped draining the Ro*Tel as an adult, and would add cumin; my friend, Mike, would doll his up with green olives, while others in our sphere would add chili or ground beef or chunks of ham.

I started experimenting with the old Chiquito style dip not long after noticing the difference once the restaurant had passed from the Donnelly clan's hands. With help from Kelley Bass and Kelly Brant, and suggestions from others, I tweaked quite a bit on the recipe. Now, when I make it, I batch it out to my mom and my friends. A pound makes a couple of containers of easy to heat, memory-jostling dip.

But when it comes to the other type, I painstakingly bake my chips from fresh tortillas, top them with cheese and beans and meat and bake again, and delicately add the avocado, lettuce, tomato, salsa, sour cream or whatever I feel like that night, onto each separate chip, usually with Hunter watching. I don't want her to ever get the idea that nachos come from a can, and hope she pressed to others the delights that are Pancho style nachos.

RO*TEL® FAMOUS QUESO DIP

1 can (10 ounces.) Ro*Tel® Original Diced Tomatoes & Green Chilies,
    undrained
1 package (16 ounces) Velveeta®, cut into 1/2-inch cubes

Place both ingredients in medium saucepan or Crock Pot. Cook over
medium heat until Velveeta is meted completely. Serve with chips.

CHIQUITO STYLE CHEESE DIP

1 stick of butter
4 Tablespoons flour
1 teaspoon paprika
1 teaspoon chili powder
1 teaspoon ground cumin
1 teaspoon garlic powder
1 teaspoon cayenne pepper

1 teaspoon hot pepper sauce
1/2 teaspoon dry mustard
1/4 teaspoon salt
2 cups whole milk
1 pound American cheese,
    cubed or sliced
    (NOT pasteurized processed)

Melt butter in a saucepan. Add flour and stir or whisk into a blonde roux
Add spices and pepper sauce, then milk, stirring constantly. Add cheese
and continue stirring until the cheese is melted and completely
incorporated into the emulsion. Remove from heat. Serve with
tortilla chips, potato chips or raw vegetables.

The Eighties were a big time for casual gatherings when there'd be pot-luck appetizers on a side table or kitchen bar for sharing while chatting. These two cracker spreads were quite common. Mom often made the ham ball and covered it with pecans or a dusting of paprika. While I see versions of both of these spreads in cookbooks of the time, it's uncommon to see them these days. I found that using the thinly sliced pastrami packets worked just as well as ham for spread, which technically doesn't make a ham ball any more, but it's what we call it.

CRAB MEAT MOLD

1 Tablespoon unflavored gelatin
3 Tablespoons cold water
1 can cream of mushroom soup
1 (8 ounce) package cream cheese

1 small onion, grated fine
1 (7 ounce) can crab meat
1 cup finely chopped celery
1 cup mayonnaise

Soak gelatin in cold water. Heat soup and dissolve gelatin into pot with soup. Add cream cheese and stir until smooth. Remove from heat, allow to cool, and fold in remaining ingredients. Refrigerated in oiled mold for eight hours or overnight. Gently invert mold onto serving dish or plate and remove mold. Serve with crackers.

HAM BALL

2 (8 ounce) packages cream cheese
8 ounces finely sliced ham or pastrami

1 bunch small green onions
1/2 teaspoon salt

Julienne ham or pastrami slices. Finely chop green onions. Fold together with cream cheese and salt. Form into a ball. Wrap with plastic. Allow to sit one hour in the refrigerator. Serve with a knife and crackers.

To make pinwheels, spread thinly on tortillas or flatbread and roll up. Slice roll evenly in 1/2 inch sections.

Of course, we've had our own potluck favorites that we throw together for gatherings now. Ours are a little different, but cream cheese stuffed peppers are very much the sort of thing I think someone would have brought to gatherings in generations before ours.

CREAM CHEESE STUFFED PEPPERS

2 (8 ounce) packages cream cheese
4 Tablespoons Parmesan cheese or Asiago cheese, grated
1 teaspoon finely grated garlic (optional)
1 bag baby bell peppers or 1/2 pound peppers of choice

Allow cream cheese to soften. Fold in cheese and garlic. Cut peppers in half lengthwise, discarding seeds. Stuff each pepper with the mixture. Refrigerate one hour.

My longtime hobby, participating in medieval re-creation in the Society for Creative Anachronism, has given me the chance to dive deep into many food cultures of the past. Over the past 30 years, I've created 15 different feasts and a host of lunches, dinners and nibbles based on research into the cuisine of dozens of places and times.

I suppose it's fitting, then, that some of those dishes have come into my usual round of foods. This particular mushroom pie recipe, a longtime favorite, was redacted from the 14th century cookbook *Le Menagier de Paris*.

MUSHROOM PIE

2 pounds mushrooms of choice (
2 Tablespoons olive oil
3 Tablespoons Worcestershire
  sauce

1 clove garlic, finely sliced
1/2 cup Parmesan cheese
1 cup Mozzarella cheese
2 pie crusts (top and bottom)

In a large skillet, heat olive oil over medium-low. Gently wash mushrooms and slice. Saute garlic for one minute, then add mushrooms and fold into pan, covering with the oil. Pour Worcestershire sauce onto mushrooms and fold again. Saute until mushrooms become soft. Remove from heat and fold in cheeses. Let cool.

Heat oven to 350 degrees. Lightly grease pie pan. Lay in bottom crust. Scoop mushroom mixture into pie pan. Press on top crust. Bake for 30-35 minutes. Allow to sit 10 minutes before serving.

From
the Bowl

I've had a love-hate relationship with onions throughout my life. When I was young, I hated everything about raw onions. I didn't know why people ate them with fish and I hated the way they made my hands rash and my eyes water.

Once I understood the true joy of caramelizing an onion, my view on them changed quite a bit. I started caramelizing onion for all sorts of things - not just for burgers and steaks but for a nice, lovely caramelized jam to include here and there.

The best use of onions for me has to be French onion soup. My favorite version is served at the Colonial Steak House in Pine Bluff. When I make it myself, I like it with roasted beef - and I love to toast my own bread for croutons, usually with melted-on provolone and mozzarella cheese.

FRENCH ONION SOUP

3 pounds onions, sliced
1 clove garlic, finely diced
1/2 stick salted butter
1 pound chuck roast or English roast, cut into 3/4 inch cubes
2 cans beef broth

1/2 teaspoon salt
1 bay leaf
2 teaspoons Worcestershire sauce
4 ounces mozzarella cheese
4 ounces provolone cheese
Croutons or bread of choice

Saute onions and garlic in butter. Once onions are translucent, transfer to Crock Pot.

Lightly salt beef cubes. Turn skillet heat to high. Sear beef cubes in skillet in turns, making sure all sides are seared. Drop into Crock Pot. Add broth and bay leaf and cover, setting Crock Pot on high. After one hour, reduce heat to low and add Worcestershire sauce. Allow to simmer 2-3 more hours until beef falls apart.

Toast bread or croutons with cheese on top, or drop cheese directly into soup and omit croutons.

68

There is something inherently comforting about a good bone broth or a delicious hot soup. This recipe is a blueprint for the chicken soup I've made over the years, guaranteed to solace the soul.

CHICKEN SOUP

1 whole chicken
2 cups diced onion, halved
2 cups diced celery, halved
2 cups diced carrot, halved
1 teaspoon parsley

1 teaspoon sage
1 teaspoon thyme
1 teaspoon tarragon
1 teaspoon salt
1/2 teaspoon black pepper

Place herbs in a muslin bag. Set chicken to boil in enough water to cover the chicken. Add half the vegetables and the herb bag. Allow to remain at a low rolling boil until the meat falls off the chicken carcass. Remove from heat and let sit 10 minutes. Pour through a wire strainer.

Separate the meat and reserve. Separate the leg and thigh bones. Break in half and return to pot with the broth.

Bring broth back to a boil. Add one bay leaf and reduce heat to medium. Allow to boil down until reduced by one quarter.

Add in remaining vegetables. Cook until tender.

Shred chicken and return to pot.

Variations:
Chicken noodle soup: 10 minutes before serving, add egg noodles to broth and allow to boil. Cut heat after 10 minutes. Refrigerate any leftovers.

Chicken and dumplings: Use the scone style biscuit recipe from earlier in this book. Instead of baking, roll out on counter and cut into 1" wide strips (or 1x2" rectangles). While broth is boiling, drop in a handful at a time. When dumplings float, remove to separate bowl. Continue to boil dumplings until all biscuit dough is used. Cut heat and return to pot when ready to serve.

Chicken and rice soup: Add 1 cup white rice and 1 teaspoon poultry seasoning to soup while broth is boiling. Cover pot and cut heat. Check 15 minutes later. Ready when rice is tender.

Medieval chicken soup: Omit celery. Add 2 cups well-washed leeks chopped in 1" sections and 2 cups cubed turnip. Add 1 teaspoon rosemary and 1 teaspoon peppercorns to herb bag. Proceed as directed.

Over the years I've spent plenty of time camping, whether in tents or rustic cabins. I've cooked over my share of Coleman camp stoves and in Dutch ovens over open fires. And I collect recipes to use that require no refrigerated items. These two soups are part of my common repertoire of camp cookables.

SOUTHWEST CHICKEN SOUP

1 can fully cooked chicken
   or one rotisserie chicken, deboned
2 cans diced tomatoes
1 can black beans
1 can corn
1/2 cup (1 small) onion, diced
   or 1/4 cup dessicated onion
3 bell peppers
   or 1/4 cup dried bell pepper

2 Tablespoons cumin
1 Tablespoon garlic powder
1 teaspoon black pepper
1/2 teaspoon salt
Choice of seasoning:
1/4 cup Cajun seasoning
   (Tony Chachere)
or 1/4 cup Creole seasoning
   (Zatarain's or Joe's Stuff)
or 1 packet taco seasoning

Place all ingredients in large Crock Pot or large stockpot over low flame and cover. Will be ready in 90 minutes but can cook as long as three hours. Serve with bread or tortilla strips.

CANNA SOUP

1 25.4 ounce bottle V8
1 can corn
1 can beans of choice
1 can mixed vegetables
   1 can diced potatoes

1 can diced tomatoes
1 can green peas
1/4 seasoning salt of choice
   (Mrs. Dash, Lawry's, etc.)

Place all ingredients (do not drain cans) in Crock Pot on low. Ready in an hour.

I spent many evenings during high school and college breaks with my friend Mark Loftin and his mom, Liz. We would often play Trivial Pursuit with other members of our cadre, including Liz's cohort, Don Barker. One afternoon, he felt compelled to instruct me on the proper making of chili. Mind you, Don felt strongly for the inclusion of beans and tomatoes in his chili, and showed me the fine tuning of the construction of this stew-like concoction, complete with the roasting of peppers over a gas flame and utilizing white pepper instead of black. My recipe differs somewhat, but it retains the base knowledge Don shared with me, a recipe I perfected by cooking up a large pot every couple of weeks in the second floor kitchen at Roush Hall on the Arkansas Tech campus, to share with my fellow dorm citizens.

CHILI

3 pounds ground chuck, browned
1 28 ounce can crushed tomatoes
1 28 ounce can diced tomatoes
4 bell peppers, flame roasted,
  skinned and diced
2 whole diced onions
1 can black beans, drained

3 cans kidney variety beans (light red, dark red, cannallini), drained
1 teaspoon white pepper
2 teaspoons salt
5 Tablespoons cumin
1 Tablespoon minced garlic
1 Tablespoon butter

Sauté peppers and onions in butter over medium heat until onions are translucent. Add garlic and sauté for another minute. Add meat, beans, and peppers and stir. Add both cans of tomatoes, cumin, and salt and stir. Reduce heat to low and let simmer for an hour or more.

I perfected my gumbo recipe over decades of visits to New Orleans and all points south of the Arkansas state line with my Louisiana friends. Gumbo can be made with most any meat. I like to use beef sausage seasoned like Andouille, chicken, and a handful of shrimp thrown in for the last five minutes. I prefer gumbo file to okra, but either will work. If you choose to use okra, put it in early so it can dissolve and thicken the gumbo without slimy strings. I use a two-roux method to make my gumbo broth nice and thick. This is the way my friend Charles Burgess enjoyed.

GUMBO

1 smoked sausage, 6 ounces, sliced
4 cups cooked chicken
1/2 cup all purpose flour, halved
1/2 cup salted butter, halved
1/2 cup or more Cajun or Creole seasoning (I like Joe's Stuff)

2 cups chopped bell pepper
2 cups chopped celery
2 cups chopped onion
1 cup broth
3 cloves garlic, finely chopped
1 Tablespoon butter

Sear sausage and chicken in a skillet. Set aside meats, leaving pan drippings. Add 1/4 cup butter and melt. Whisk 1/4 cup of flour in, creating a roux. Continue to whisk until roux reaches a dark chocolate color. Immediately dump in onions, celery and bell pepper and fold through the roux, completely coating the vegetables and stopping the roux cooking process. Slide vegetables into stockpot and pour in broth. Set pot over medium heat on back burner. Saute garlic in one tablespoon butter and add to stockpot.

Once again, add 1/4 cup butter to skillet and whisk in 1/4 cup of flour until the roux is blonde. Slide into stockpot. Add meats and seasoning, stir until incorporated, and cover. Allow to bubble away 2-3 hours. Serve over rice, French bread or potato salad. Gets better with time.

There's a good deal of crossover in what is considered native cuisine between LA (Louisiana) and L.A. (Lower Arkansas). Both places have a reverence for the simple, rich stick-to-your-bones meal of red beans and rice. While it's considered a Monday food in many places, all I need to consider whipping up a batch is a hankering for comfort food and a busy night ahead. It's ridiculously simple. Just be sure to stir every time you walk by.

RED BEANS AND RICE

1 pound small red beans
6 cups water
2 Tablespoons Creole seasoning
1 teaspoon salt
1 bay leaf
1 onion, diced

2 cloves garlic, diced
1 pound Cajun sausage, sliced
2 Tablespoons Crystal or Panola garlic pepper sauce
2 cups broth (chicken or beef)
Choice of seasonings to taste

Bring water to boil. Add beans, bay leaf, Creole seasoning and salt. Cover and reduce heat to medium for 30 minutes or until beans have soaked up most of the liquid. Sear sausage with onion and garlic until onion is translucent. Add to pot with pepper sauce and broth. Stir and cover, occasionally returning to stir again, over a minimum of 90 minutes, adding water or broth when beans soak up the liquid in the pot. Best with four hours cook time. Serve over rice.

Colder weather calls for Settlers Beans. Forget pork-n-beans; this combination of meat, beans and tangy sauce was a hearty stick-to-your-ribs dish that could stand on its own for dinner. It was also something my mom made for potlucks. The dish always came back empty.

SETTLERS' BEANS

1 pound ground beef
1 large onion, chopped
1 pound bacon
¼ cup brown sugar
½ cup sugar
½ cup barbecue sauce

½ cup ketchup
4 Tablespoons sorghum molasses
2 (16 ounce) cans navy beans
2 (16 ounce) cans pork and beans
2 (16 ounce) cans chili beans

In a skillet, brown ground beef and onion. In another skillet, fry bacon. Drain both. In a stockpot, stir together brown sugar, sugar, barbecue sauce, ketch-up and molasses. Add in beef, bacon, onion and beans and simmer on low heat for at least one hour.

Thick soups are versatile - you can make them up as-is, put them under potatoes for a shepherd's pie creation, or pour them into a crust and cover them for pie. This one here's great to make with leftover Thanksgiving turkey.

CHICKEN OR TURKEY POT PIE or SOUP

3 cups cooked turkey or chicken, chopped no more than 1/2 inch

2 cups turkey broth from pan or 2 cans broth

1 cup water

1 cup each diced carrots, onions and celery or one 12 ounce bag mirepoix frozen mix

1 bay leaf

1 can potatoes sliced potatoes

1 can corn

1 can green beans

1 cup milk

1 cup flour

2 teaspoons poultry seasoning

1 teaspoon white pepper

1 teaspoon black pepper

1 teaspoon salt

1 double crust pie crust

Set Crock Pot to low. Combine in Crock Pot the broth, water, mirepoix, bay leaf, and turkey. Add pepper(s), salt and poultry seasoning. Stir well. Add potatoes, corn and green beans *and the liquid in the cans*.

Make a slurry with the milk and flour and add it to the Crock Pot. Stir all well. Cook on low 7-9 hours (overnight works well). Remove bay leaf. Allow to cool completely before serving or baking.

To bake: Heat oven to 350 degrees. Spray or wipe down your choice of three pie plates or one 3 quart or larger casserole dish. Line dish(es) with pie dough and blind bake for 25 minutes. Remove from oven. Add in pot pie filling, cover with remaining crust and bake for 35-45 minutes. Remove from oven and allow to sit for at least 10 minutes before serving.

Things
Noodles
go with

I have yet to find out why chicken spaghetti and turkey tetrazzini have different names. I've encountered both all over Arkansas, and the recipe tends to be very close to identical with the exception of the meat that is used. This is good with chicken or with leftover turkey from my roasted turkey recipe.

TURKEY TETRAZZINI or CHICKEN SPAGHETTI

2 cups cooked and diced turkey
    or chicken, shredded
1 can (10.75 oz.) cream of chicken or cream
of mushroom soup
1 can-full (10.75 ounces) reserved homemade broth or 1 can broth
1/4 cup chopped onion
2 Tablespoons diced pimento
1 teaspoon dried parsley or 2 teaspoons fresh parsley
1 4 ounce can mushrooms
1 cup water
8 ounces uncooked spaghetti
1 cup shredded cheese
salt, pepper and spices to taste

Turn your standard Crock Pot to high. Place onions in pot and assemble other ingredients. Once the onions start to become translucent, add the soup, broth, parsley, pimento, mushrooms, and water. Stir well.

Break spaghetti noodles in half and add them to the Crock Pot, making sure they are submerged. Add the turkey and cheese and stir. Taste and add salt, pepper, poultry seasoning or other spices to taste.

Turn Crock Pot to low and let cook for one hour. Taste for seasoning, add spice of choice and let cook up to three hours more. Let cool completely.

HINT: If you are making this recipe and aren't making it from a turkey you seasoned and roasted yourself, taste and season the meat before adding to the Crock Pot.

Maybe I heard it wrong. But years ago, one morning after I got off work, when Paul and I were watching Food Network and chilling out before bed, Mario Batali was chatting the guests up on his show and mentioned timbolo. As he described the dish, I realized it was something I'd been making for years. Now it had a name. Think of it like baked ziti - except it's not necessarily ziti. It's something to make when you have a number of different complimentary items, some sort of sauce and some sort of pasta. Timbolo was, for many years, a Thursday or Friday morning dish containing parts of other dishes I'd made through the week. Best part was, because of the consistency, it was sliced like lasagna.

TIMBOLO

3-4 cups cooked pasta (any noodle)
1 cup sauce of choice (marinara, meat sauce, Alfredo pesto)
1 cup of fully cooked proteins

1 cup of vegetables
1-2 cups of mozzarella
1/4 cup Parmesan cheese
1 egg (optional)

Proteins:
ground beef
ham
bacon
ground sausage
link sausage
shredded chicken
shredded turkey

Vegetables:
pitted olives
zucchini
tomatoes
eggplant
mushrooms
onions
bell peppers

Heat oven to 350 degrees. Make sure all protein and vegetable pieces are less than 1/2 inch in size. Mix proteins, vegetables, half of cheese, egg (if using) and sauce together. Fold in cooked pasta. Turn out into 2 quart covered baking dish and top with remaining cheese. Place cover on dish and bake at 350 degrees for 35 minutes. Remove cover and bake an additional ten minutes. Let cool 10 minutes, then cut and serve like pie.

MEDITERRANEAN VEGETABLE SIDECAR

1 fresh zucchini, sliced
1 fresh yellow squash, sliced
2 medium tomatoes, cut in wedges
1 bell pepper, diced
1 medium onion, diced
1 clove garlic, crushed

2 Tablespoons olive oil
1/2 teaspoon oregano
1/2 teaspoon parsley
1/2 teaspoon thyme
1 teaspoon Cavender's Greek
    Seasoning (optional)

Combine herbs and seasoning and shake together. Toss vegetables together with herb mix.

Heat oil in a skillet over medium heat. Drop in vegetables and garlic and stir to coat with oil. Continue to lightly stir as vegetables cook. Remove when tender. Serve alongside any Mediterranean dish.

ROASTED GARLIC

3-4 bulbs garlic
2 Tablespoons olive oil
1 teaspoon salt

Heat oven to 400. Slice tops off garlic bulbs, just at the top edge of the cloves. Spread open a little with your fingers, like you're opening a blossom.

Place garlic bulbs in an oven safe bowl just big enough for the bulbs. Carefully spoon olive oil into bulbs. Lightly salt the tops of the bulbs.

Roast in oven at 400 degrees for 45 minutes. Remove from oven and cover bowl with foil. Serve with crusty bread and more olive oil alongside your favorite Mediterranean dinner.

ROASTED ITALIAN VEGETABLES

2 tomatoes, cubed
1 zucchini, cubed
1 medium onion, diced
1 yellow bell pepper, diced
10 black olives, sliced

10 green olives, sliced
2 Tablespoons olive oil
2 teaspoons balsamic vinegar
Cracked black pepper to taste

Heat oven to 400 degrees. Toss all vegetables in oil and place in 9x9" glass square baking dish. Roast in oven for 25 minutes.

Remove from oven. Drizzle balsamic vinegar over top and pepper the dish. Perfect for antipasto or as a side dish.

I have been to most every Greek Food Festival at the Annunciation Greek Orthodox Church here in Little Rock, back to when it was just a tiny community event where my friends danced and yelled "opa!" while I enjoyed way too much baklava. I have grown to love the community, learned much about the fantastic church and its members, and spent so much time in its kitchen. The operation and coordination of the crew that puts together tens of thousands of pastries over the course of the five months ahead of the festival is truly breathtaking.

When it started, it was nigh on impossible to find gyros or sourota around here, unless you actually knew a Greek family. Today, there are lots of ethnic restaurants that serve most of those delicacies offered at each year's festival, but as far as I've been able to tell, only one restaurant I know of offers my favorite - pastitsio. The combination of delectable and subtle spicing and bechemel sauce layered with noodles truly has my heart. And, when given the time, I can make the dish myself.

PASTITSIO

Meat Filling:

2 pounds ground beef, lamb or blend of both
1/2 cup olive oil
2 cups chopped onion
1 (14-ounce) can tomato sauce
3 tablespoons fresh parsley, chopped
3/4 teaspoon ground allspice
1 teaspoon ground cinnamon
Salt and pepper to taste
1/4 cup breadcrumbs

Pasta:

1 pound bucatini, perciatelli or elbow macaroni
1/2 teaspoon salt
1/2 cup (1 stick) unsalted butter
4 egg whites (reserve yolks)
1 1/2 cups Parmesan cheese

Bechemel Sauce:

1 cup (2 sticks) unsalted butter
1 cup all-purpose flour
1 quart milk (warmed)
8 egg yolks (beaten lightly)
Pinch ground nutmeg

Gather all ingredients before you begin.

Put a pot of water on the back of the stove and set to boil.

Heat olive oil in a large skillet. Add ground beef and onions cook over medium-high heat until the pink color disappears.

When the water begins to boil, add the pasta and 1/2 teaspoon salt.

Add tomato sauce, parsley, allspice, cinnamon, salt, and pepper and allow the sauce to simmer over low heat for 10 minutes. Stir breadcrumbs into meat sauce to absorb excess liquid. Remove from heat.

Check the noodles. When al dente, remove and drain through colander. Let sit to cool.

Return pasta pot to back burner. Melt butter in it. Drop the noodles back in it and toss to coat. Fold in beaten egg whites and Parmesan cheese.

Grease a lasagna pan or casserole dish with olive oil. Layer half the pasta into the bottom. Press down to flatten. Add the meat mixture in an even layer. Top with remaining pasta noodles and press down.

Heat oven to 350 degrees. Heat the milk in the microwave for two minutes, or warm to body temperature in a saucepan.

Melt butter in the skillet that you cooked the meat in. Whisk in the flour to make a roux, but don't let the roux darken more than slightly yellow. Whisk in milk in splashes keeping the sauce smooth. Let it bubble slightly over low heat, but do not let it boil. Once it thickens, remove from heat and fold in beaten egg yolks and nutmeg.

Pour bechemel over the noodles, making sure to get the sauce over the entire surface of the dish. Sprinkle with Parmesan. Bake at 350 degrees for 45 minutes or until the bechemel begins to turn golden brown. Let stand at least 15 minutes before serving.

83

POZZA'S PASTA
HANDMADE ITALIAN LINGUINI

I've found myself in Shreveport quite often throughout my life. On one post-SCA event evening, my friend Sara Willis suggested we try this place called Monjuni's - and boy, I am glad she did. See, I hadn't had a nice, sweet marinara for a very, very long time - and Monjuni's sauce hits all those notes I had missed.

On my last visit before the pandemic set in, I picked up a jar of the sauce to savor at home. This summer, I brought home two cases of tomatoes from a family farm outside Warren, one of Bradley County Pinks and one of Cherokee Purples. They were huge, and many "got ate" quick. Still, a week later, I still had most of a case of tomatoes left. So I went for making sauce. Thus was born a nice, lovely bounty of pomodoro sauce - which had that same lovely sweetness as Monjuni's sauce.

POMODORO SAUCE

12 pounds tomatoes
1 Tablespoon olive oil
1 pound sweet bell peppers, diced
1/2 pound fresh onion, finely diced

4 cloves garlic, thinly sliced
1 ample handful fresh sweet basil
1/4 cup sugar
1 teaspoon salt

In a large stockpot, scald tomatoes, then peel them and cut them into quarters, removing any hard stem bits. Set aside. In the same stockpot, saute onions and sweet bell peppers in olive oil. Once the onions are translucent, add the garlic and the tomato wedges, stir together and let cook 5 minutes.

Blend together all vegetables in the pot with an immersion blender, then dust with sugar and salt and stir. Add in sweet basil and simmer 20 minutes. Can using a pressure cooker. Makes four pints. Serve with pasta or with crusty Italian bread for dipping.

Kat Robinson

Everyone has a movie or two that influences their lives. I've had a few, but just one that's directly related to my foodwriting. It's not something cool like *Hiro Dreams of Sushi*, or something dark like *The Cook, The Thief, His Wife and Her Lover*, though there are... merits to both.

The movie is *Ratatouille*. It's beautiful and sweet and contains a marvelous adage of "anyone can cook." As a food writer, though, one simple, single moment sticks out - the moment when critic Anton Ego takes a bite of the eponymous dish and is transported back to childhood.

I've had those moments. I treasure them. And while I'd been writing about food for three years before I saw the movie, the idea of that moment set in with me like a beacon. I don't write about just the food. I write about what emotions a flavor or experience brings to a person.

That being said, when summer's oppressive humidity and ever-present sun lays heavy across the air, the flavors I crave comes from my native soul. A blister of heat, a dollop of sauce, and slices of every vegetable I encounter comes together in a dish that's an amalgamation of every summer side item.

RATATOUILLE

2 pounds various fresh Arkansas vegetables:
    tomatoes, zucchini, eggplant, onion, yellow squash, bell peppers, any
    and all varieties
1 cup mushrooms (optional)
2 cloves garlic, finely diced
1 handful fresh parsley, finely chopped
1 handful fresh basil, finely chopped
1 cup olive oil
1 teaspoon salt
1 cup tomato-based sauce (spaghetti, pomodoro, marinara)

Slice all vegetables and mushrooms thinly. Stir together garlic and salt in olive oil and lightly toss all vegetables and mushrooms within.

Heat oven to 350. In an oven-safe casserole dish, dollop half of tomato based sauce into bottom. Carefully stand slices of vegetables on end, alternating between different types to showcase color and variety. Once done, drizzle remaining sauce over top. Bake uncovered for 35-45 minutes until vegetables reach desired firmness. Serve alone or over pasta or bread. Can also be a delightful side dish. Cover and refrigerate leftovers.

Leftovers can be incorporated into pasta primavera the next day or served as a cold salad with a drizzle of vinaigrette. They can also be dropped onto a crust with red sauce and cheese for pizza.

87

STUFFED BELL PEPPERS

4 whole bell peppers
2 teaspoons salt, divided
1 pound ground beef, turkey, chicken, lamb or pork)
1 clove garlic, sliced
2 Tablespoons chopped onion
1 teaspoon black pepper
1 teaspoon basil (optional or substitute with Italian seasoning)
1 1/2 cups cooked rice
1 cup Parmesan cheese
2 8-ounce cans tomato sauce
4 ounces (1/4 pound) Provolone cheese, sliced

Cut bell peppers at top of pepper, in a circle around the stem at the edge of the side of the pepper. Remove and discard seeds and white bits. If there's bell pepper cut with your stem, slice it off and chop it.

Bring enough water in a pot to cover the peppers to a boil, adding one teaspoon salt. Place peppers in boiling water with tongs, making sure to fill the cavities with the water. Allow to boil for five minutes. Remove from water with tongs. Drain upside down.

Heat oven to 350 degrees. In a skillet, brown ground beef with onion, garlic, and any reserved chipped bell pepper. Season with basil, salt and pepper.

When beef is fully cooked, fold in rice and reduce heat. Add in one of the cans of tomato sauce and fully incorporate. Remove from heat and add Parmesan cheese.

Place peppers in baking dish. Add a slice of provolone cheese to the bottom of each pepper. Fill peppers with meat mixture. Pour over remaining can of tomato sauce. Top each pepper with a remaining slice of Provolone cheese.

Place in 350 degree oven and bake for 30-40 minutes or until cheese is browned. Serves 4.

Parallel foodstuffs fascinate me. Like bread pudding and French toast, meatloaf and meatballs share so much in common. I can pretty much whip up either one with so many different items, that the recipe for each is more formula than exact instruction. The biggest difference between my meatballs and my meatloaf is the sauce - but both can be made with traditional Italian seasoning, Indian-style garam masala, or any other flavor profile you'd like to try. Any time I need to make a meal for the masses, meatballs are usually on my advance prep list, and they freeze well.

MEATLOAF or MEATBALLS

1 pound ground beef or pork
2 cups filler (cooked rice, cooked oats, crushed crackers, breadcrumbs)
1 egg, beaten
1 Tablespoon seasoning (Italian seasoning, garam masala, or other blend)
1 onion, finely diced (optional)

Heat oven to 350 degrees. Mix together filler and seasoning. Mix together egg, meat and onion. Mash together both mixes and incorporate.

For meatballs: Line a 13x9 baking pan with foil. Roll 1.5" balls from the meat blend and place in pan, touching but not tight. Bake 25-30 minutes or until internal temperature reaches 155 degrees. Remove from oven, scoop meatballs from pan and place on mesh or small grid wire rack to cool.

For meatloaf: Line a baking sheet with foil. Spritz with cooking oil. Form entire mass of meat into a loaf approximately 8x10". Place in center of pan. Smear half of sauce on top. Bake 45-55 minutes or until internal temperature reaches 150 degrees. Remove from oven and allow to rest for 20 minutes before serving. Serve with remaining sauce.

Meatloaf sauce: Mix together 1 cup ketchup, 1/4 cup honey, 2 Tablespoons Worcestershire sauce and 2 Tablespoons cumin.

The poorest I have ever been as an adult has been the last year I spent in Jonesboro. The significantly small check that came with being a small market TV producer at KAIT, combined with the overambitious choice of renting a large house and my boyfriend's part-time hours, car expenses and inflation culminated in about six months of hand-to-mouth survival that left us with very little to survive on once bills were paid. I learned I could go to Country Mart, get one of those boxes of cheap hamburger patties for $5, and spend the rest on noodles, tomato sauce and spices to make a batch of spaghetti that would get us through the week. The spaghetti diet sucked, but it kept us from building debt at a time we couldn't pay it back.

That's when I learned a big batch of spaghetti sauce was cheaper when you brought it together yourself.

SPAGHETTI

2 cloves garlic, finely chopped
1 medium onion, diced
1 cup chopped celery
1 pound ground beef
1 small can mushrooms, diced
1 6 ounce can tomato paste

1 15 ounce can tomato sauce
1 teaspoon oregano
1/2 teaspoon salt ·
1/2 cup Asiago or Parmesano
Romano cheese, grated
1 pound cooked pasta

In a heavy stockpot, brown ground beef together with mushrooms. Drain and return to pot. Add celery, onion and garlic and fry together until onion is translucent. Add in paste, sauce, oregano and sauce. Stir and reduce to simmer.

When sauce has reduced by one quarter, add in half the cheese. Stir until cheese is fully incorporated and remove from heat.

Sprinkle pasta with the remaining cheese and toss. Spoon over sauce.

With meatballs: Omit ground beef and saute together onion, celery, garlic and mushrooms in 1 Tablespoon butter. Continue as directed. When you add the cheese, add the fully cooked meatballs (see recipe previous page) and allow 10 minutes to soak up the flavors of the sauce before serving.

Baked spaghetti: Heat oven to 350. Once sauce is prepared, fold in pasta (and meatballs, cooked chicken or cooked sausage if desired). Spray a 2 quart covered casserole with olive oil, then lay in the spaghetti and cover with the other half of the cheese. Bake covered for 20 minutes, then uncovered 15 minutes or until cheese begins to brown. Serve hot.

A Dinner of Fried Chicken

A single piece of fried chicken can be the make or break of a first impression or even a relationship. Conquering such an uncomplicated dish is a benchmark for cooks, one not reached so often in this modern age.

Pan fried single batter chicken was a thing of my youth, as was Shake-N-Bake ("and I helped.") and baked chicken and stewed chicken and, well, chicken. Once a special meal prepared for important company, the chicken has become the common denominator of quick and cheap dinners, the tofu of meats. You can do almost anything to chicken.

The simple pan-frying of my childhood was watching a woman (didn't matter which grandmother, aunt, family friend or stranger) first dunking chicken parts into a batter of flour, buttermilk and spices and then laying it in two inches of Crisco bubbling hot in a cast iron pan. The secret of when to turn the pieces, how to do so without knocking off the batter and knowing when it was done was a gift one earned. I sure as hell didn't get it, not until I was into adulthood.

For that, I blame the chicken nugget. Well, fast food chicken in general. The first Magic Meal was conjured at Wes Hall's Minute Man when I was just a few years old; the McDonald's combo meal followed. Kentucky Fried Chicken was already in Benton when I was there as a toddler. Chicken nuggets, while attributed to Robert C. Baker of Cornell University, were first documented in 1971 in a recipe by Searcy native Norma Young, whose Dipper's Nuggets won that year's National Chicken Cooking Contest. A version first appeared on the menu at McDonald's in 1980, and quickly made their way to other restaurants.

By the time I was cooking, the needed knowledge of properly frying chicken was superseded by the availability of quick and easy pick-up options. Learning how to fry chicken wasn't as important as learning to fry fish - because you couldn't (and still can't) get fried black bass or crappie through a drive-through.

I made attempts, sure, during my later college years when I shared a duplex apartment with five other people off South Houston in Russellville. They weren't good attempts. The meat had no flavor, the crust would fall off, or each piece would have a nice outside and a raw, inedible interior.

My breakthrough came, like so many things, through cooking in the Society for Creative Anachronism. I came across a recipe for brined and buttered baked chicken, and decided to use it for my second medieval feast, a fete that would become a 268 person dinner in February 2001. One night of a salt and sugar brine, one hour baking after a butter basting, and I had one of the most amazing roasted chicken dishes I'd ever tried. The next step was to take it to the skillet - which I did, happily.

I've continuously refined the recipe since then, picking up bits of information from Alton Brown on *Good Eats*, at the Viking Cooking School, and just by asking so many of the people I have interviewed over the years.

No one in Arkansas was surprised when the BMF (buttermilk fried chicken) at The Hive at 21c in Bentonville was named the best fried chicken in the nation by *Men's Journal*, because it was made by a marvelously talented Arkansas chef who knew his business. Few outside our state are surprised that it's good here. Through decades of roadside diners offering the dish to passers-through, generations of Italian cooks in Tontitown refining theirs to go alongside spaghetti at the annual Italian Feast, soul food cooks preparing and serving it up at David Family Kitchen in Little Rock or Rhoda's Famous Hot Tamales in Lake Village... we do chicken well here in Arkansas.

Soon it'll be Hunter's turn to learn the art. I'm thrilled to be able to share a decent recipe with her. I'm also sorrowful - because when I went to make this fried chicken in July 2020, to take photos for this book and to document this recipe, I screwed up. I pride myself on being able to go anywhere in our state and find good food. But this one day in the kitchen ruined me for fried chicken. It was so perfect, from the flavor of the meat to the spice and consistency of the crust, that I just hate to say, I prefer my own now. Sorry, chefs. I'm ruint.

FRIED CHICKEN

You can make this up with any part of the chicken you like - but really, if you're not frying chicken thighs what are you doing with your life?

1 pint buttermilk or yogurt	2 Tablespoons paprika, halved
1 pint pickle juice	2 Tablespoons dried parsley, halved
2 Tablespoon pepper sauce, divided (Crystal garlic pepper sauce)	2 Tablespoons garlic powder, halved
4-5 pounds chicken thighs	2 teaspoons salt, halved
2 cups large breadcrumbs from toasted bread	2 teaspoons black pepper, halved
4 cups flour, divided	6 eggs
	Vegetable oil or Crisco for frying, enough for an inch in a skillet

The day before, combine buttermilk or yogurt, pickle juice and 1 table-spoon pepper sauce in a pitcher. Divide chicken out into two ziptop gallon sized bags. Pour half of the pitcher's contents into each bag. Press out all the air from each bag and seal. Massage the brine into the chicken. Place in refrigerator.

The next day, pour the entire batch and chicken into a large colander and let it sit while you prep the fry.

Place in one ziptop bag three cups of flour and one tablespoon each paprika, parsley, and garlic powder.

Place in another a cup of flour, a cup of breadcrumbs, a tablespoon each of paprika, parsley, garlic powder, and a teaspoon each salt and pepper.

Make up a bowl of four eggs and a tablespoon of pepper sauce. Beat the eggs into the pepper sauce.

Heat oven to 350 degrees.

Bring your oil in your skillet up to medium high heat, somewhere in the 375-400 degree range. Salt and pepper your chicken lightly, with the re-mainder of each. You're ready to begin.

Take your chicken and place it in the first bag. Shake the hell out of it. Pull it out, dunk it in the egg bath, and put it in the second bag. Shake it again. Take chicken out and gently lay it into that hot oil. Brown both sides. Let drain on a rack. Repeat with the rest of the chicken.

Get your oven heated to 350 degrees. When all of your chicken is fried, move to a rack on a baking sheet and put that baking sheet in the oven. Bake for 35-45 minutes or until your chicken has reached an internal temperature of 155 degrees.

Pull out and let rest for 20 minutes. It will come to full temperature, and it'll be good. It's even better the next day cold out of the fridge

One of the many assignments Grav and I tackled over the years is fair food. My guide to all the eats at the Arkansas State Fair has become a yearly standard that television and radio folks share out, no matter their affiliation. We've also, between the two of us, covered fairs of all sizes in six other states, including Alaska for Grav and Missouri for me, along with Texas, Tennessee, and Louisiana.

The hardest assignment is, without a doubt, the State Fair of Texas. Known for its famed fried foods contest, the annual celebration in Dallas brings so many new food items, it takes a full day to just shoot, try and document all we can find. We've had some remarkable dishes there. We've also had some truly awful ones.

The first year we went, 2010, was the year of fried beer. Now, fried Coke started a trend of frying beverages, and most drinks are fried by pouring them in funnel cake batter. Not fried beer. Someone had the bright idea of freezing beer down below zero, then popping it into ravioli casings and sealing them. When an order is placed, the frozen beer ravioli is thrown in the deep fryer for a minute and served immediately. Biting into one brings forth a splash of flat, cool beer. It tastes approximately like a belch.

The second year was far worse. In 2011, the winner of the most unusual fried dish at the fair was fried bubblegum. Grav was appalled, but I was intrigued. It couldn't be that bad, right? I mean, it was just bubblegum flavored marshmallows, coated in bubblegum flavored batter, deep fried, drizzled with bubblegum flavored frosting and served topped with Chick-lets.

It could be exactly as bad as it sounds. Worse, even, was the fact that the flavor wouldn't go away. We continued our sojourn through fairlands, photographing and trying dish after dish. We consumed super spicy Cheeto balls, odd flavors of ice cream, even fried margaritas with their dousing of tequila. Nothing could expunge the cloying aftermath of a single bite of the noxious dessert. Nothing, that is, except a gratefully consumed Greek salad, the roughage of lettuce finally pulling the permeating nastiness from our palates.

But what does this have to do with Arkansas and its food? There's a dish that was introduced at the Arkansas State Fair a few years ago, a delicacy that we first encountered at that State Fair of Texas, that was proclaimed to be the first ever of its sort anywhere. I sadly had to explain to the vendor in question that, while the idea was unusual, it was not unique.

The dish in question? Fried chicken skins.

Mind you, fried pork skins are part of the culinary fabric of this state. You can find them on store shelves, at bait shops and convenience stores, even as a bit of lagniappe at restaurants. Our Mexican groceries serve chicaronnes in so many way, including these huge foot-wide takewiths that seem like they should be on a fair's midway on their own.

But fried chicken skins? They deserve the best of what fried chicken has to offer, which is the crust. For folks who eat fried chicken JUST for the crust, this is a no-brainer. For those who eat fried chicken for the chicken, step back a couple of pages.

That recipe works just as well on chicken skins, too. If you have chicken you're cooking and remove the skins, save them back in the freezer for a fun experiment - and for chicken gravy, which is the delicious end-product of this creation.

FRIED CHICKEN SKINS

Skins from 5-10 pounds of chicken breasts or thighs, approximately 1 pound

1/2 cup buttermilk	1/2 teaspoon pepper
1/4 cup pickle juice	1 cup large breadcrumbs from
2 cups flour, divided	toasted bread
2 teaspoons parsley	2 eggs, well beaten
2 teaspoons paprika	1 teaspoon cayenne garlic sauce
2 teaspoons garlic	Vegetable oil or Crisco, enough for
1/2 teaspoon salt	an inch in the skillet

Place skins in a gallon sized ziptop bag. Add buttermilk and pickle juice and massage into skins. Press the air out of the bag, zip and set aside.

In a second ziptop bag, place flour and all dry spices. Shake until combined thoroughly. Divide and put half in a third ziptop bag. Add breadcrumbs to the third bag.

Beat together the eggs and the pepper sauce. Bring oil or Crisco to popping heat in skillet.

Open first ziptop bag. Two or three skins at a time, dump the skins into the second bag, shake well, dunk in the egg bath, then dunk into the third bag and shake well. Immediately place in hot grease and allow to fry until golden brown, turning once to toast other side. Remove to paper towel lined plate. Serve with pickles, Ranch dressing, chow chow or what you like, or use to crumble into chicken gravy.

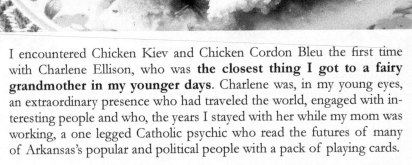

I encountered Chicken Kiev and Chicken Cordon Bleu the first time with Charlene Ellison, who was **the closest thing I got to a fairy grandmother in my younger days**. Charlene was, in my young eyes, an extraordinary presence who had traveled the world, engaged with interesting people and who, the years I stayed with her while my mom was working, a one legged Catholic psychic who read the futures of many of Arkansas's popular and political people with a pack of playing cards.

Charlene often took me places I probably would not have visited as a child otherwise. We once took a trip to New Orleans to pick up a new prosthetic leg. I came along as her navigator, reading the maps put together in a three ring binder for her by a travel agent friend. We stayed out in Metarie but she made sure to drive me into the city so I could have my first peek at Bourbon Street and we could enjoy cups of gumbo a block off Lafayette Square.

I was also often her dining buddy, and it was with her that I visited a posh French restaurant where waiters were dressed in finery, where I could back away from the windows looking out over Little Rock (due to my fear of heights), and where I could enjoy remarkable dishes. That restaurant was Jacques and Suzanne's.

My version of these two dishes isn't as grand as what you'd discover in such a fine dining atmosphere, but they're easy enough for the home cook, which is certainly more my aesthetic.

CHICKEN KIEV or CHICKEN CORDON BLEU

Butter shapes for Kiev:

1/2 pound (2 sticks) unsalted butter
1 teaspoon salt
1/2 cup chopped fresh parsley
1/4 cup chopped fresh tarragon
1 clove garlic, finely chopped
1/2 teaspoon lemon juice (optional)

Incorporate all ingredients. Make an inch thick roll of the soft butter on wax paper, then roll up (it does not need to be perfect). Freeze.

OR - Cordon Bleu-ing:

1/2 pound ham or turkey ham, sliced to 1/4 inch, rind removed
8 ounces Swiss cheese

Cut cheese into four equal sections. Roll ham slices around Swiss cheese.

Chicken:

4 boneless chicken breasts
1 teaspoon salt
2 eggs, beaten
1/2 cup flour
2 cups breadcrumbs (Panko)
2 Tablespoons olive oil

Heat oven to 400 degrees.

Slice breasts 3/4 way through from one side to the other, and lay open. On a firm surface, pound breasts skin side down with a mallet until a uniform thickness around 1/2 inch. Lightly salt both sides.

Either remove herbed butter from freezer and cut into four sections, or have your ham-wrapped Swiss cheese sections ready to go. Wrap chicken around butter shapes or ham rolls, pulling chicken firmly around each and securing it by piercing the chicken edges with a toothpick, making sure the edge is folded tight. The chicken must completely fold around or it will not work and you'll have seepage.

Set up bowls, one each with flour, egg and breadcrumbs. Place each breast in the flour and roll, making sure to cover every part. Dip each breast in egg, completely coating, then carefully roll in breadcrumbs. Set on plate and allow to rest while skillet is heated.

Heat a skillet to medium and pour in olive oil. Place each stuffed breast in the hot oil with tongs and allow to cook three minutes each side, until the crust has darkened and the chicken has sealed.

Place on baking sheet lined with foil (for easy cleanup). Bake for 14-16 minutes - you'll hear the chicken fat sizzle. Remove from oven and let rest five minutes. Serve within 30 minutes. Expect no leftovers.

103

MASHED POTATOES

2 pounds potatoes (skin on or off, your choice, quartered
1 teaspoon salt

1/4 cup heavy cream
1 stick butter, melted
Salt and pepper to taste

Cover potatoes in stockpot with an inch of cold water. Add salt. Set burner to high and allow to boil 15-20 minutes or potatoes are tender. Drain.

Mix together heavy cream and butter. Pour into stockpot. Blend with hand mixer right in the stockpot, until potatoes are desired consistency. Taste and season as you wish.

CREAMED POTATOES

2 pounds potatoes, skinned & cubed
2 teaspoons salt

1 cup half and half or heavy cream
1 teaspoon black pepper

Boil cubed potatoes and salt covered by an inch of water until the water reaches the potatoes. Drain remaining water.

Add cream and black pepper, then use an immersion blender and blend to a soft paste right in the pot. If potatoes are still too stiff, add more cream or milk.

If you don't have an immersion blender, put boiled potato cubes, cream and pepper in a blender and pulse until desired consistency.

BEEF OR CHICKEN WHITE GRAVY

1/2 cup flour
1/2 cup chicken or beef drippings
1-2 cups milk

1/2 teaspoon salt
1/2 teaspoon pepper
Beef bits or reserved chicken crust

Heat drippings in a skillet over medium flame. Whisk in flour to make a roux. When the roux reaches a dark tan, add in a cup of the milk. Continue to whisk until fully incorporated. Add salt and pepper.

If gravy is too thick, add more milk in splashes, incorporating with a whisk. When to desired consistency, remove from heat and fold in beef or chicken bits.

This works great with the fried chicken skins recipe.

One of the things I did when I was working for the Arkansas Department of Parks and Tourism was assisting other journalists who came into the state for stories. I was doing just that with a writer with the Society for American Travel Writers on a trip to Historic Washington State Park, when I encountered this dish from childhood at Williams Tavern Restaurant. It's a delightful, bright dish that goes well with both hot meals and summer plates.

BLACK-EYED PEA SALAD

1 can black-eyed peas, drained
1 can green beans
1 medium chopped onion
¾ cup chopped red bell pepper
¾ cup chopped green bell pepper
1 seeded jalapeño, minced (opt.)

3 green onions, chopped
¼ cup minced fresh parsley
1 jar (2 ounce) minced pimento
1 garlic clove, minced
1 cup fat free Italian dressing

Combine all ingredients and toss gently. .Refrigerate for 24 hours.

I could, at one point in my life, shell peas with the best of them. So many Saturday afternoons in June at Grandma Bear's were spent with a basket between my feet and a bowl in my lap. These were days of grabbing handfuls of PurpleHull pea pods, pinching the end of each one open, running my thumb along the inside and letting the peas fall into the bowl, the pinging of the first peas against the metal bowl subsiding to quiet pops as the bowls filled. You worked all the pods you'd picked up until they were done, then pulled them out of the bowl and shoved them into a paper Piggly Wiggly sack. The pods would turn your thumbs purple, and no amount of scrubbing would get the color out from under your thumbnail. Peas were put up in the freezer, to be enjoyed year-round cooked with chunks of ham or bacon and served as a side dish or just with cornbread.

CROCK POT PURPLEHULL PEAS

2 pounds shelled PurpleHull peas
4 ounces smoked meat (ham, bacon, turkey, chicken, whatever)

2 Tablespoons meat drippings
2 Tablespoons Creole seasoning
1 teaspoon salt

Place all ingredients in Crock Pot and stir. Heat on high for 20 minutes, then turn to low and let simmer for 1-2 hours.

You know in the movie *Kung Fu Panda*, where it's revealed that the secret ingredient of Mr. Ping's soup is nothing? Or, more succinctly, "there is no secret ingredient, there is only you." Sorry if I spoiled that for you, but where have you been?

The secret ingredient in so many cookbooks from our churches and clubs is... missing.

When I started digging through said cookbooks that I've collected over the ages, I noticed this - whether it was the lack of cheese in a cheese dip recipe or a vegetable dish that seemed to be missing a spice, it's been common. I suspect it's because there have always been some cooks who don't want to share all of their secrets.

For so many of those vegetable dishes, the missing ingredient is chow chow, a piquant condiment once created from end-of-season vegetables that needed to be utilized, which when soaked in spices and vinegar created a marvelous spoonful of wonder to add to any savory dish. I like it in corn, beans, peas, salad dressings, with chicken, fish, anything, really.

CHOW CHOW

2 heads of cabbage, sliced thin
8 cups green tomatoes, chopped
8 cups onions, chopped
8 cups assorted bell peppers, chopped
1/4 cup salt
5 cups sugar
4 Tablespoons whole grain mustard
1 Tablespoon turmeric
1 Tablespoon mustard seed
3 Tablespoons celery seed
1 Tablespoon ground ginger
1 teaspoon ground coriander
1/2 teaspoon allspice
1/2 teaspoon ground cloves
1/2 teaspoon red pepper flakes
1 cinnamon stick
2 bay leaves
10 cups vinegar of choice

Place all chopped vegetables in bowl, cover with salt and refrigerate overnight

Place all remaining ingredients in a large pot and bring to a boil, then simmer for 10 minutes. Remove bay leaves and cinnamon stick.

Rinse and drain the vegetables, then add them to the pot. Stir until all the vegetables are well coated and hot - but do not return to a boil.

Pack the chow-chow into hot, sterilized half-pint jars, leaving 1/2 inch head space in jar. Clean the rims, then place lids and ring on top. Leave the rings loose. Use pressure cooker method to seal.

109

Comfort
Eating

I loved the idea of eventually going to France as an adult. There was something about the romantic nature of the country, particularly with its dishes, that appealed to me. I suspect some of that came from growing up in a state with ties to French explorers, to being in the city named for a small formation on the Arkansas River called La Petit Roche, and having Julia Child amongst my Saturday morning chefs to watch. I gravitated towards whatever I could find French for a while, and spent three years learning the language in high school.

Of course, when I started cooking in the SCA, I delved into some of the most marvelous surviving texts of the age, particularly *Le Viandier de Taillevent* and *Le Ménagier de Paris,* a couple of 14th century French cookbooks. These, more than Child's body of work, engaged my mind and my belly.

That being said, though I love my cookbooks, I tend to more cook along the methods and flavors I've fallen in love with - which means when one has apples and leeks, a big pot of chicken thighs is begged to me bade.

CHICKEN WITH APPLES AND LEEKS

2-3 pounds chicken thighs
2 Tablespoons butter
1 teaspoon salt
1 teaspoon white pepper
1/2 cup flour
2 leeks, thoroughly washed
    and chopped into 1" sections
1 cup chicken broth

1 tablespoon and one teaspoon
dried thyme, divided
1 teaspoon parsley
1/2 teaspoon sage
1/2 teaspoon oregano
2 apples, cut into 1" cubes
1 cup half-and-half

Heat Dutch oven over medium high flame. Rub chicken thighs with salt, pepper and one teaspoon of the thyme. Placing skin side down, sear until brown, then flip and sear other side. Remove from Dutch oven.

Add butter to chicken drippings and melt. Make a roux with the drippings and the flour, bringing it to a tan color. Add in leeks and toss together until roux stops browning. Add in chicken broth and remaining spices. Stir all together and heat until bubbling.

Heat oven to 375 degrees. Fold apples and half-and-half into contents of pot, then add chicken and fold over again. Bake in oven for 55 minutes. Remove from oven and allow to stand, still covered, for 15 minutes before serving. serving.

There's one singular flesh-and-starch combination that I have seen in just about every culture I have ever studied - that of poultry and rice. Think about it - are there any cultures that don't have some version of the combination as am important part of their cuisine?

Here in Arkansas, it's one of the most common things, in so many variations thanks to our farmers. Arkansas is the second largest producer of chicken in the United States, and our state produces more rice than all other states put together. Something I took for granted as a child was just how much these two things came together.

The easiest dishes were the ones I learned early on - putting a chicken in a pot of water, boiling it to done then throwing in rice and spice and letting it bubble away until solid, pick out the bones and eat. That spice might have just been poultry seasoning and sage, or an added can of cream of mushroom soup and black pepper. It could be made in the hour before I went to work overnight wherever I was going, whether it was an overnight radio shift or a TV morning show shift. I would get up, wash the chicken, boil the water, shower, get dressed, throw in the rice, watch a little TV, pull out a Tupperware container and scoop enough out for my overnight lunch, put the rest in the fridge and have some before going to bed. It was enough for me and Paul both, those years we were dating and working the same place, and after we married and were heading to our respective stations for our competing morning shows.

Chicken is such a cheap protein, it does so well to meet the budget. I once edited a healthy cooking magazine special with approved recipes meant to meet slim budgets and feed four people each while providing enough nutrients to survive the day. All but three of the entrees in the meat section were chicken-based.

So I guess it's no wonder I spent so much time experimenting with it, particularly with rice. I can whip up almost anything with some chicken, some rice and an hour or less. They're simple and useful. You can also use turkey, if it's what you have. Here ya go.

PARMESAN CHICKEN or TURKEY RICE

2 cups chicken or turkey, cooked
  and shredded
1 cup white rice
1 chicken bouillon cube

2 cups water
1 cup broth
1 tablespoon Parmesan cheese
1 teaspoon dry parsley

In a four quart or larger pot, set water to boil. Add chicken and rice mix
or white rice and chicken bouillon cube. Stir well. Bring to a boil, then
reduce to a simmer for five minutes.

Add turkey and broth, and let simmer until broth has been absorbed
by the rice. Remove from heat. Stir in cheese and parsley. Add side of
choice. Serves four.

CHICKEN LOAF

1 pound ground chicken
1 small onion, diced
1 cup white or brown rice, cooked

1 egg
2 Tablespoons Italian seasoning
1 tablespoon poultry seasoning

Heat oven to 350 degrees. Bring all ingredients together in a bowl. Spray
a 9x9" glass square dish with oil. Press chicken mixture into dish.
Bake at 350 degrees for 40 minutes. Let stand 10 minutes, then
serve with chicken cream gravy.

HAWAIIAN FRIED RICE

1 pound uncooked chicken, cubed
1/2 pound ham, diced
1 onion, chopped
1 Tablespoon vegetable oil
2 Tablespoons soy sauce

1 8 ounce can pineapple chunks
1 Tablespoon brown sugar
3 cups cooked rice
1/2 teaspoon black pepper
3 eggs

In a bowl, cover chicken and ham in soy sauce.

Saute onion in vegetable oil. When the onion is translucent, add chicken and ham with sauce into pan. Add entire can of pineapple with juice. Fry over medium high heat until chicken is fully cooked and sauce has thickened.

Add brown sugar, pepper and rice and incorporate until rice is no longer white.

Clear a spot in the middle of the skillet. Crack eggs and drop into the cleared spot. Once eggs begin to fry, fold into rice and continue to cook, folding frequently, until eggs are cooked.

Turn fried rice out of pan into bowl. Serves 4-6.

TERIYAKI-STYLE CHICKEN AND FRIED RICE

1 pound boneless chicken,
  cut into 1" pieces
1/2 cup soy sauce, halved
1/4 cup brown sugar
1/4 cup mirin or michiu
2 cloves garlic, crushed
1 inch ginger root, grated

2 Tablespoons vegetable oil
2 cups cooked rice
1/2 cup chopped onion
2 eggs
1 package frozen Asian vegetables
  (optional)

Mix together half the soy sauce and the brown sugar, mirin, garlic and ginger. Marinate chicken for an hour in the blend. Drain well.

In a hot skillet, heat vegetable oil. Place chicken and onion and cook through. Add in rice and toss together. Splash in soy sauce and fold into rice.

Clear spot in skillet and drop in two eggs. When they begin to fry, fold into the rice. Add vegetables if using. Toss until rice is uniform color and vegetables are covered. Serve immediately.

SESAME GREEN BEANS

1 package frozen green beans
  or two cans green beans
1 teaspoon cooking oil

1 Tablespoon sesame seeds
1/4 cup sesame oil
2 Tablespoons brown sugar

Heat oil in skillet. Mix together sesame oil and brown sugar. Pour green beans into skillet. Add sesame oil and brown sugar blend and sesame seeds. Toss and heat until beans are coated and slightly tender.

The first time I tried a curried dish in an Indian restaurant, I cried. It was 1995. My boyfriend took me to Star of India and insisted I try the vindaloo, since that's what Dave Lister loved so much on *Red Dwarf*. I wasn't prepared for the rather hot, bold spicing and broke into tears. Bless his heart, Sami Lal came over and asked what was wrong and asked me if I'd like to try something different. A few minutes later, he returned to our table with a mild chicken tikka korma. I was apprehensive, but on first bite I realized I'd found something really marvelous.

I started studying different sorts of Indian and Pakistani food shortly thereafter. Learning about regional and historical cuisine led me to start experimenting with my own curries and the spices that went into them. I learned that the whole idea of curry powder came from the English, specially designed to replicate flavors of India once countrymen who had been stationed on the subcontinent returned to their home in the British Isles. I learned how to cook directly from toasting spices on up.

Making curry this way takes a lot of time and patience. So... I also make curry powder with toasted, dehydrated and ground spices, to suit my own tastes. You may not have the time to go through the efforts of toasting and crushing your own spices. If you do, contact me and we'll talk curry. If you're really just wanting some tasty eats now, here's a quick curry you can whip together in your own kitchen.

KAT'S QUICK CURRY

1 pound chicken, cubed
  (dark meat is better)
8 ounces yogurt
2 Tablespoons turmeric, halved
2 Tablespoons cumin, halved
1 Tablespoon ground garam masala
1/2 teaspoon salt

1/4 teaspoon ground coriander
1/4 teaspoon pepper
2 Tablespoons ghee or butter
1/2 cup half and half
  or coconut milk
3 Tablespoons honey (optional)
1-2 teaspoons chili sauce (optional)

Place chicken, yogurt, a tablespoon turmeric and a tablespoon cumin into a gallon sized ziptop bag. Massage yogurt and spices into the chicken. Place in refrigerator for two hours before cooking. Drain and let sit in colander five minutes before cooking.

Mix together remaining turmeric and cumin along with other dry spices. Toss chicken in spices. Heat ghee in skillet. Drop chicken into hot ghee and stir fry, making sure to heat all sides of chicken. Add half and half or coconut milk, along with honey if you want it sweet or chili sauce if you want it hot (or both). Stir and cover, reducing heat to medium low (curry should slightly bubble). Allow to cook chicken through and sauce to thicken. When chicken is done, serve with its sauce over rice or with naan.

The summer plate is an Arkansas tradition that is overlooked by our peers in the culinary world, but which deserves an explanation and joy unto itself. It bears as little tie to exact description as "a picnic" or "a buffet," being based more on its enaction than its contents. The short description is a cold meal served at midday during the summer months, featuring fresh local fruits and vegetables. But it can be many more things - which is why both the plate on the left and the plate on the right qualify.

There's no set tradition recorded for posterity (unless you count my references in previous books or the few articles that have born their own fruit over the past several years). Ask any Arkansawyer whose past includes rural life, and they'll nod and share their favored items. The idea behind the dish appears to date back to our pre-air-conditioned days, when it was verboten in many homes to turn on the stove and thus head up

the house. Remnants of previous meals, vegetables and fruits picked that morning, pickles, cornbread and such were offered up for sharing, with each diner choosing their own portions. It was a way to both quickly consume a repast with no additional cooking and a chance to consume a variety of items in one meal, offering a chance to salve the satiety of each at the table.

Is there a right or wrong way to construct a summer plate? Again, definition does not suffice here. Whether yours includes cold fried okra and pan fried potatoes, pepper relish with cold peas, thick slices of tomatoes or cantaloupe, crunchy raw onion or fresh cucumber, the summer plate is whatever you make it, and deserves the celebration it is due.

Enjoy your own bounties each summer, and think of the delights best brought to table in this simple meal.

The
Catfish
Feast

Is there a more Arkansas meal than the catfish feast? It's a meal celebrated with countless dinners, festivals, and get-togethers of all sorts, and its compiled ingredients are assembled in a way that's particular to our state.

The construction of the meal varies little, wherever it's served. Its components are simple - cornmeal-encrusted catfish, hush puppies, brown beans, green tomato relish, coleslaw, chunk of white onion, wedge of lemon. The pattern is repeated at so many of our restaurants, where the catfish is purchased by the piece and the fixings come with it. Some offer a set-up of the side items, plenty to make a meal on their own.

The condiment of choice is the green tomato relish, more succinctly pickled green tomato wedges that are both sweet and salty while being mildly piquant. There are individuals and even a few restaurants that accompany the selections with seafood cocktail sauce or tartar sauce, but I haven't a clue why.

The other condiment that comes to table is hot sauce. Commercial products like Tabasco sometimes show up, but the general consensus is that the pepper sauce should be the vinegar in which whole or sliced peppers have soaked for an expanse of time. The pepper sauce goes on the fish, in the beans, wherever you like it, just like that spritz of lemon or that white onion that's bitten into with whatever bite ends up on the fork.

Hush puppies themselves are a source of friction, whether they should be savory or sweet, filled with bits of corn or onion or even jalapeno, or just plain. The name for the lumps of cornmeal batter is reportedly the cause of porch dogs, who would beg until you gave them something. Since catfish frying is usually conducted outside, placating the pups is of importance.

If you are out and about in The Natural State and see a seafood restaurant, nine times out of ten that restaurant is a catfish joint. Even though catfish never come from the sea, their ties to water merit the idea, however misguided it might be. Some restaurants only serve catfish; others offer frog legs, fried chicken and whatever else comes about.

I have caught my share of channel cats in my life, and blues too. I've had more than one back fin spear me in the hand. Catfish grunt when you pick them up out of the water, talking with their whiskers and flailing with intent to injure. They don't go down without some fight. These ornery bottom dwellers come with skin instead of scales, and their eggs in recent years have become a source for a poor man's caviar, God only knows why.

I've found myself steeped in catfish culture all my life. I know what it's like to go down in the bottoms and how to pull a trotline, and that the best bait for catfish is the stinkiest stuff you can find, or raw cuts from another fish.

When clean and fresh, they're excellent. I don't care for them much when they're muddy - that is, when they have a muddled, gamey flavor - but most folks I know who eat catfish enjoy them that way.

First weekend of June 2000, I was invited up to judge a catfish cooking contest for the first time. I was the morning show producer at THV in Little Rock, and my new husband had the same job at KARK across downtown. We both ended up getting the invite, which our anchors had sidestepped and passed on to us. We get out to Jacksonport State Park for Portfest, and there's just a few of us judging. The organizer asked us to choose whether we wanted to judge the traditional or nontraditional contests. Well, of course with my curiosity, I went for the non-traditional. And I experienced bites of catfish I'd never conjured - catfish and corn casserole, teriyaki catfish, catfish gumbo and even smoked and barbecued catfish. I was so blown away by all the combinations. Paul, on the other hand, got to judge 22 different plates of fried catfish against each other. He went on a catfish strike for years after that.

There are other ways to enjoy catfish, sure. I cook it sometimes like my mom showed me, broiling it with lemon juice and a dash of Tabasco. I have tempura battered it and served it with pickled radish, made fish cakes and even tried to almandine it - that wasn't so successful. But I like it best with a rice and flour batter, with a little coleslaw and some butter toasted French bread. I don't make it often, though.

Knowing the components of a catfish feast is important to anyone who wants to claim themselves an Arkansawyer, so here are the parts of that feast, in these several pages.

FRIED CATFISH

2 pounds fresh catfish fillets
2 cups milk
1 teaspoon pepper sauce
2 cups yellow cornmeal
½ cup all-purpose flour

1 teaspoon salt
½ teaspoon ground black pepper
1/4 teaspoon garlic powder
1/4 teaspoon cayenne pepper
Peanut or canola oil or Crisco

Rinse catfish and place in bowl. Add milk and pepper sauce and set aside.

Mix together everything else except oil or Crisco in a wide bowl.

Put two inches of oil or Crisco in a deep skillet and heat to high.

One at a time, lay catfish fillets in cornmeal mix, pat down, flip, pat down again and remove to hot oil. Fry fish two or three at a time, leaving an inch between the pieces. When one side is browned, use a wide metal spatula and carefully flip to other side. When done, remove to paper towel covered plate to drain. Cook hush puppies in the same oil.

127

RICE FLOUR FRIED CATFISH

2 pounds fresh catfish fillets
2 cups milk
1 teaspoon pepper sauce
2 cups rice flour
1/4 cup all-purpose flour
  or almond flour

1 teaspoon salt
½ teaspoon white pepper
1/4 teaspoon garlic powder
1/4 teaspoon cayenne pepper
1/4 teaspoon parsley
Peanut or canola oil or Crisco

Rinse catfish and place in bowl. Add milk and pepper sauce and set aside.

Mix together everything else except oil or Crisco in a ziptop bag.

Put two inches of oil or Crisco in a deep skillet and heat to high.

One at a time, place catfish fillets in ziptop bag, shake well, and remove. Place in hot oil with metal spatula. Fry fish two or three at a time, leaving an inch between the pieces. When one side is browned, carefully flip to other side. When done, remove to paper towel covered plate to drain. Cook hush puppies in the same oil.

HUSH PUPPIES

1 cups cornmeal	4 teaspoons sugar
1 cups flour	2 large eggs, slightly beaten
3 Tablespoons baking powder	1/4 cup milk
1/2 teaspoon salt	1 cup chopped onion (optional)

Combine dry ingredients. Beat milk and eggs together and add to dry ingredients. Blend together until combined. Fold in onion and any leftover batter from catfish.

Drop by tablespoonfuls into hot oil and fry until golden brown, about four minutes.

Variations:

Corny hush puppies: Omit milk,. Add one can cream-style corn.

Warm hush puppies: Add 1 four ounce can diced Mexican chilies.

Hot hush puppies: Add two finely diced jalapenos.

Cheesy hush puppies: Add one cup grated cheddar cheese.

Hunter and I have traveled much of her life. Back in 2015, we drive the entire length of Scenic Arkansas Highway Seven, the longest of our state highways. The night we stayed at DeGray Lake Resort State Park, Hunter and I had dinner at the Fish Nest Family Restaurant nearby. She ordered a kid's meal, but when the set-up for my dinner came out, she went to town, eating an inordinately large number of hush puppies and gobbling down two bowls of brown beans... after which she passed out without even touching her chicken and fries. That night in our room at the state park, it sure got windy.

BROWN BEANS or PINTO BEANS

2 pounds pinto beans

1 Tablespoon butter

1 medium onion, diced

3 cloves garlic, minced

1 teaspoon black pepper

2 cups broth

1 ham hock, smoked turkey leg, half a pound of bacon ends or 1 cup beef jerky (optional)

Put pinto beans in a 12 quart or larger stockpot. Cover with two inches water. Let soak overnight.

The next day, drain and set aside in separate bowl. In the same stockpot, melt butter. Saute onion and garlic, then add broth and, if using, smoked meat. Add beans and stir. Put top on pot and let simmer 4-6 hours.

PEPPER SAUCE

2 pounds peppers of any sort - jalapeno, cayenne, poblano, serrano, pequin, banana, any variety, keeping in mind the pepper's heat
Up to a quart of apple cider vinegar

Remove stems and seeds from peppers. Pack as tightly as possible in any size jars (pints are usually best).

Bring vinegar to a boil. Pour over peppers in jar. Cap, shake gently to remove air, take top off and put it back on again, leaving ring loose. Seal in pressure cooker, or sit in sunny kitchen window. Let stand one month. After opening, you can keep this jar in the fridge or on the table.

To utilize, either transfer peppered vinegar to cruet or bottle, or use a dropper to pull vinegar from jar and deposit on food. Peppers are also great as a float in chili, or diced and used in any hot dish.

Coleslaw's not an extraordinary dish in itself, but when paired with chicken or barbecue, it's downright essential. The fresh, cool bite pairs beautifully with hot catfish and provides a great counterpoint to brown beans, cools off a hot sauce bite and gives crunch to the whole meal.

There are two schools of thought on coleslaw - those who believe coleslaw should be creamy, and those who think it should be soaked. Level of sweetness is also a consideration, since different slaws range from neutral to Kentucky Fried Chicken slaw sweet. This first recipe is beautifully colored, creamy and bright and is more along what I make today. The second recipe comes from Nana, my maternal grandmother, and is best after spending time in the freezer. They're both quite good - the latter, though, is surprisingly sweet for what's in it.

CREAMY COLESLAW

1 head cabbage (for color, half red, half green), thinly sliced
2 carrots, shredded
2 bell peppers, diced
2 cups mayonnaise
1/4 cup whole grain mustard
1/4 cup apple cider vinegar
1/4 cup sugar
2 teaspoons celery seeds
1 teaspoon salt
1/4 cup pepper

Toss together cabbage, carrot and bell pepper. Mix all other ingredients together, and toss vegetables in sauce. Refrigerate one hour. Serve cold.

COLESLAW FOR FREEZING

1 medium head cabbage, shredded
1 teaspoon salt
1 carrot, grated
1 bell pepper, chopped
1 cup vinegar
¼ cup water
1 teaspoon whole mustard seed
2 cups sugar
1 teaspoon celery seed (optional)

Mix cabbage and salt. Let stand one hour. Squeeze out excess moisture. Add carrot and pepper.

Combine vinegar, water, seeds and sugar in saucepan and bring to a boil for one minute. Cool to lukewarm. Pour over vegetables. Pack in one quart containers and freeze until needed.

Fried green tomatoes just weren't a part of growing up for me, not until the 1980s and the movie *Fried Green Tomatoes at the Whistlestop Cafe* based on the book by Fannie Flagg came out. I remembered Fannie - I watched her on Match Game with my grandmother sometimes. But that movie changed what we did with some of those falls.

By falls, I mean the tomatoes that were still green that would drop from the plant, usually while we were picking. Frying them didn't occur to us. If you knocked one off, you took it inside and set it on the windowsill until it reddened. If you found it off the plant, you carefully rolled it over and made sure no insect had already burrowed its way inside. If it had insect holes or rot, that was good practice for pitching. I got really good at overhanging slightly rotten green tomatoes out over the fence. You didn't do it with the red ones that had fallen because they could come apart in your hand and then that was a mess.

Falls were summer. Actually picking green tomatoes was what happened when that first autumn frost was predicted. Grandma Bear had so many rows of tomatoes, we would hustle and pull and bring everything in, red or green. The red ones that weren't eaten quickly were put up as sauce.

The green ones, though, went into the pot with vinegar, sugar and spices. They would become that marvelous creation that pairs so well with fresh-caught fried crappie or catfish. **I grew to love green tomato relish so much I'd eat it by itself, a small bowlful when I had the chance. I still do.**

GREEN TOMATO RELISH

2 quarts quartered green tomatoes
2 cups chopped onion
1/3 cup chopped hot peppers
1/3 cup chopped red bell peppers
1/3 cup celery, chopped
2 cups sugar
3 Tablespoons salt
3 cups apple cider vinegar
1 teaspoon celery seed
1/4 teaspoon mustard seed

Combine ingredients in a large pot and bring to a slow boil. Let simmer for about 5 minutes. Ladle into hot, sterile jars, wipe lip edge of jars, screw on hot, new jar rings and flats and lightly tighten. Place into a boiling water bath, with at least 1/2 inch of water above the jar lids. Bring to a boil; keep slowly boiling for 15 minutes.

Remove and let cool overnight, then label and store for at least two weeks.

CHICKEN FRIED GREEN TOMATOES

2 green tomatoes
1 cup flour
1/2 teaspoon paprika
1/2 teaspoon dill
1/2 teaspoon garlic powder

1 cup breadcrumbs, finely crushed
1/2 teaspoon salt
1 egg
1 teaspoon pepper sauce
Oil for frying

Slice tomatoes 3.8" to 1/2" thick.

In a ziptop bag, place all dry ingredients and shake. Divide into second ziptop bag. Add breadcrumbs to second bag.

Beat egg with pepper sauce.

Heat 1" oil to medium high.

One at a time, shake tomatoes in flour mix bag, dip in egg wash, shake in breadcrumb bag and place on waiting plate. Lay tomatoes into oil in sets of three or four slices. DO NOT overfill the pan or allow tomato slices to touch. Cook 10 minutes each, turning at the midway point. Drain, cool, eat.

If you're making a large mess to be served all at once, cook a total of six minutes, just browning both sides. Remove to metal rack over a baking sheet. When you have filled the sheet, place in a 250 degree oven for at least 10 minutes or up to 45 minutes. Rest 10 minutes and serve with choice of dip.

LIGHTLY FRIED GREEN TOMATOES

2 green tomatoes
1 cup all-purpose
  or rice flour
2 teaspoon salt
1/2 teaspoon pepper
Oil for frying

Slice tomatoes to no more than 1/2 inch thick. Place other three ingredients in ziptop bag and shake to incorporate.

Heat an inch of oil to high. One at a time, shake tomato slices in bag with flour mixture, pull out and lay into hot oil. Don't crowd the pan, but place 3-4 slices in to fry at a time. Remove to paper towels for draining. Let cool a few minutes before eating.

CORNMEAL FRIED GREEN TOMATOES

2 green tomatoes
1 cup finely ground cornmeal
1 cup all purpose flour
Salt and pepper
1 egg
1 teaspoon pepper sauce

Slice tomatoes no more than 1/2 inch thick.

In a ziptop bag, combine the cornmeal, flour, salt and pepper.

Beat egg together with pepper sauce in bowl.

One at a time, dip tomato slices in egg wash, then shake in cornmeal mix bag. Lay into hot skillet of oil at medium high heat. Cook eight minutes, turning midway. Drain.

I've never met a tomato I didn't like. Any color, any size, the fruit of the tomato vine is the one food I think I could quite possibly not live without. It's fortunate, then, that I live in Arkansas, where both the state fruit and vegetable are the Bradley County Pink Tomato. And before you cite an objection over that particular distinction, you need to get yourself a Bradley County pink. What, you haven't had one? Then you just can't fully understand why our legislature made such a choice.

That being said, I should point out that the same varietal has been taken other places, namely California and Mexico, and grown for crops that go to grocery stores. Those tomatoes, so uniform, are picked green for shipping and never quite get the flavor right. A true Bradley County pink tomato is grown in lower Arkansas, varies in size and bears a marvelous salt and savor flavor that defines garden umami.

The best way to eat a Bradley County pink is over the kitchen sink. The second best way is on a white bread sandwich with a little butter and mayonnaise or Miracle Whip. Some swear by a BLT but, as is evidenced by this here photograph, the tomato slices sometimes overwhelm the bacon and always overshine the lettuce.

But those tomatoes aren't our only stars. Healthy, dark Cherokee purple tomatoes grow well in the same soil, as do colorful varieties of grape and cherry tomatoes, Big Beefs and Better Boys, Pink Brandywines and Arkansas Travelers, all appearing each year from June to the first frost, gorgeous and delicious and right here at the right time. My daughter, like I did before her, snacks on them no matter their size. Big fat slices appear on burgers and sandwiches, small ones pop up in salads and so many go into the pots of sauce stirred by our Italian descendants and the typical home cook. The intent is to consume them at their peak, when they're ripe and burgeoning with robust flavor.

139

Cornbread, Corn, and Things to Give Thanks Over

To say cornbread has been part of my life is... well, it's rather apparent, I'd think. Outside of the traditional hillbilly stereotypes you hear about my state, there are a few things that ring true - **a love of big brimmed hats, denim, and cornbread.**

It was, and in many places still is, the great grain, the staple beside our repasts, the humble bread beside our beans, our greens, chunks of ham or bowls of stew, a goulash sopper, a soup soaker, a way to paste a repast to the bones within. Never muffin-sweet but not bereft of sweetness, either. My mom likes sugar in hers. Nothing wrong with that, as long as you don't let it get away from you, like the corn muffins sometimes included in my daughter's junior high school lunch, from a California company which holds pride in its organic products but knows nothing of the grit and chew of Arkansas cornbread.

The trick to a good cornbread lies in the heat of the skillet or pan it goes into. There's something about the nice crust formed by browning up the butter a bit before the batter goes in, which holds together the slice and brings just a touch of sweetness to the entire affair all on its own. I find myself sometimes sauteeing onions in that butter before the pourover, omitting the sugar for honey, and serving up mine with a fat pat of parsleyed or garlicked butter on top.

Papaw Bruce, my maternal grandfather, worked for Reynold's Aluminum most of his life. He was a third shifter, a trait my mom as a nurse and me as a television producer would emulate in later years. Papaw would come in and, for his morning supper, eat cornbread out of a cup. His cornbread received a pourover of buttermilk or sweet milk before he dug into the cup with a spoon. Satisfied, he'd retreat to the front bedroom to sleep. Us grandkids, whichever were there, were shooed out to the yard to entertain ourselves. As I grew older, I learned that my ability to keep quiet and busy myself with reading the thick volumes of The Book of Knowledge earned me a place indoors, especially wonderful when the summer heat was oppressive.

Of the cornmeal dishes I've encountered throughout my life, Mom's Mexican Cornbread stands out. I would happily dig in to every slice. She would make up a recipe of regular cornbread but, once half the batter was in the pan, she'd cover it with creamed style corn, sharp cheese and some sort of pepper - usually chopped jalapenos she kept in a pull-up Tupperware container from the refrigerator door. When it came time to go through the recipes here, while I was still unable to handle the weight of the cast iron skillet, she made up a batch just so I could take a photo. I coveted every bite of the slice on my plate.

CORNBREAD FROM A MIX

2 Tablespoons salted butter
2 cups self-raising cornmeal mix
1 1/2 cups buttermilk or milk

2 eggs
1-2 Tablespoons sugar
  or 1 Tablespoon honey

Heat oven to 425 degrees.

Beat together eggs, buttermilk milk and sugar or honey. Fold in cornmeal mix and stir until smoothed.

Heat 10 inch cast iron skillet on the stove to high. Drop in butter and allow to melt until foamy. Roll the skillet or use a brush to push it up the sides. Pour in cornmeal batter and let fry for a moment, then stick the skillet in the stove and leave it there 20 minutes. Check to see if a knife comes out clean; if not, cook an additional five minutes. Once it's out, allow to cool five minutes before cutting. Cover leftovers.

MAKE YOUR OWN MIX

1 cup all-purpose flour
1 cup cornmeal
2 teaspoons baking powder

1/2 teaspoon baking soda
1/2 teaspoon salt

Shake or sift together well before using in this recipe.

MEXICAN CORNBREAD

2 Tablespoons salted butter
Batter from cornbread recipe previous page
1 can creamed corn
1 can green chilies or 1/2 cup chopped peppers of choice
4 ounces sharp cheddar cheese
1/4 cup pimentos or onions, chopped (optional)

Heat oven to 425 degrees.

Heat skillet over high flame. Add butter and brown, rolling pan to coat sides. Pour in half of batter. Spread cheese over batter, then cover with creamed corn and remaining ingredients. Pour remaining batter over the top. Remove from heat and place in oven uncovered.

Cook 25-30 minutes at 425 or until top browns. Pull out and allow to sit 10 minutes before serving.

SWEET CORN MUFFINS
for those who absolutely want sweet, fluffy cornbread

1 cup cornmeal
1 cup all-purpose flour
2 teaspoons baking powder
½ teaspoon salt

1 cup sugar or 3/4 cup honey
1 egg, beaten
¼ cup canola oil
1 cup milk

Preheat oven to 400 degrees. Grease 12 count muffin pan. Place in oven.

In a large bowl, mix together dry ingredients. Add remaining ingredients and stir together.

Pull hot muffin pan out of oven Spoon batter into each cup. Bake at 400 degrees for 15 to 20 minutes, until inserted knife comes out clean.

Fine for eating with soup or stew. Or, split open, butter and drizzle with honey for a sweet snack.

QUICK SWEET CORN CASSEROLE

1 batch sweet corn muffins
1 can creamed corn

1 egg
1 cup milk

Break up corn muffins into small pieces. Beat together egg and milk. Add creamed corn and muffin bits. Pour into greased 2 quart casserole dish and bake at 350 degrees for 40 minutes. A great side dish when you can't think of anything else to fill this space.

At Thanksgiving, the job of carving the turkey usually falls to me. I usually just process half the turkey before we sit down - a breast cut of white meat beautifully sliced on top of a pile of hand-pulled dark meat usually comes to the table for immediate dining. The remainder gets processed after we're done, and immediately separated out into containers. Carcass becomes soup, white meat and dark meat go into tetrazzini, pot pie, soups, sandwiches, and turkey salad. Nothing goes to waste.

ROASTING A TURKEY

1 turkey, 6-9 pounds
1 pound salted butter
1 bunch fresh parsley
2 cloves garlic, finely chopped
1 bunch fresh sage

1/2 cup coarse salt
2 cloves garlic, crushed
1/2 cup olive oil
2 apples or pears sliced in half

In advance - mix room temperature butter with garlic, parsley, and sage. Place in butter molds or small (2-4 ounce) bowls. Freeze butter shapes.

Be sure to thaw any turkey according to instructions (if turkey was frozen).

To prepare turkey, set oven to 350 degrees.

Remove turkey from packaging. Set aside giblets and neck. Rub bird vigorously with salt, inside and out. Mix crushed garlic and olive oil, then repeat rub inside and out.

Within, place fruit. Wrap wing tips with aluminum foil. Place in French casserole or roasting pan and put in the oven.

After one hour, open oven and pull out rack. Rub butter shapes on bird, then place remaining butter shapes on the breast of the turkey and slide back into the oven. Reduce temperature to 275 degrees. Cook another hour to three hours until internal temperature reaches 155 degrees. Remove from oven, cover with aluminum foil and allow to rest 20 minutes before carving. Discard fruit.

CORNBREAD DRESSING

1 batch cornbread (any recipe)
1 raw onion, chopped
2 sticks butter
1 cup cooked grits
1 cup chopped pecans

2 eggs
2 cans cream of chicken soup
2 Tablespoons poultry seasoning
1 teaspoon sage
Salt and pepper to taste

In a skillet, sauté onion in two sticks butter. Pour into Crock Pot.

Break up cornbread into crumbs into Crock Add all other ingredients. Stir.

Cook on low heat in Crock Pot for two hours, stirring occasionally. Serve as a side dish, or stir in chicken or turkey and serve as entrée.

Kat Robinson

SWEET CORN

Dumas, Arkansas

870-382-5738

Triple Sweet Yellow & White
Picked Fresh Daily

www.esausweetcorn.com

Corn is a normal, natural part of our diet here, and not just with corn-bread. We don't grow as much as Iowa or Nebraska, but you'll still find thousands of acres planted in the Arkansas Delta, and smaller plots here and there throughout the rest of the state.

The most famous corn you can find here is Esau's Sweet Corn, from the Esau farm near Dumas. The family operation started in 1990, and the star of their harvest is Triple Sweet. You can reserve bags each year beginning May 15th for pickup. Several farmers' markets across the state offer it, but it goes quick.

ESAU'S SWEET CORN ON THE COB

4 ears Esau's Sweet Corn

Shuck off the outside husk of each ear, leaving a full layer of inner husk. Break off the stem and the top of the ear near the silk. Place on a plate and microwave four minutes. Peel away husk and silk. Repeat if you have more than one person eating, as many times as necessary. Serve hot.

ESAU'S SWEET CORN OFF THE COB

Take the previous corn on the cob recipe and cut the corn off the cob with a knife. Serve hot.

ESAU'S SWEET CORN IN THE FREEZER

Prepare the corn on the cob as before, but except for microwaving, put four or five ears into each gallon ziptop bag. Press out air. Put in freezer. Keeps up to a year, though you'll probably want to pull it out for Thanks-giving or Christmas and show everyone else how smart you are to have stuck back this good corn.

CAVENDER CORN

4 fresh ears corn   Cavender's Greek Seasoning

Shuck cobs and break in half. Generously season with Cavender's Greek Seasoning. Place in Crock Pot over high heat. Cover and let sweat one hour.

CORN AND TOMATO SALAD

10 ears sweet corn, shucked   2 large tomatoes, finely chopped
1/4 cup olive oil   1 medium red onion, diced
1 teaspoon salt   12 fresh basil leaves, thinly sliced
3/4 teaspoon pepper   1 cup Italian salad dressing
3/4 teaspoon red pepper flakes

Preheat oven to 400 degrees.

Brush corn with oil. Bake corn uncovered for 10-12 minutes, or until corn begins to brown. Remove from oven and allow to cool. Cut from cobs.

Mix together salt, pepper, pepper flakes, basil and salad dressing. Layer 1/3 of the corn, half the tomatoes, half the onion, 1/3 of the corn, the other half of the tomatoes, the other half of the onion, and the rest of the corn. Drizzle the dressing mixture over all, making sure to cover the entire surface of the corn. Refrigerate at least 20 minutes before serving. Can be made a day in advance..

Having a non-traditional schedule can bring you to making odd food choices. That's the way it was for me when I worked at KARN Newsradio, KAIT and THV on the overnight shift. Lunching when everyone else is asleep meant I was in a weird world of bring-from-home or sneak downstairs and eat junk from the vending machine while watching out for the weird guy working in the telecomm section.

One of my better choices, at least as far as satisfaction went, was choosing broccoli, rice and cheese for those long stretches. After a while, it also became a common potluck dish.

BROCCOLI CHEESE CASSEROLE

1 cup rice (white or brown)
3 cups water
1/2 teaspoon salt
2 cups broccoli

8 ounces American cheese, sliced
1 can cream soup (chicken, mushroom, broccoli or celery)
1/2 teaspoon pepper (optional)

Bring salt to a boil in two cups of the water. Add rice and cook until tender. Once rice is cooked, remove from heat and add soup and 1 cup water.

Heat oven to 350 degrees. Place broccoli in bottom of casserole dish. Top with half of the cheese. Scatter broccoli over the cheese, then top with remaining cheese and black pepper.

Bake at 350 degrees 25-35 minutes. Allow to stand 10 minutes before serving. Serves 8. To reheat, heat for 45-60 seconds in the microwave for a single serving.

I like dried cranberries, but I'm not a big fan of cranberry sauce. I suspect it's some early childhood memory tied to the way the sauce slides out of a can, its similarity to canned beets, and getting the two things mixed up. Beets, particularly canned beets, are at the bottom of the list of things I will put in my mouth.

I'm not big on the French's fried onions and cream of mushroom soup version of green bean casserole, either, which I'm sure pleases my brother to no end. Zack can make a dent in a green bean casserole.

This dish combines two things I want to like in a way that satisfies me.

GREEN BEANS WITH CRANBERRIES

1 package frozen or two cans drained green beans	1/4 cup almonds, chopped
	1 Tablespoon butter
1/4 cup cranberries, chopped	Salt to taste

Heat butter in skillet over medium flame until it begins to brown. Add in cranberries and almonds and toss until both are coated and the aroma blossoms. Add in the green beans and toss again. When the beans are heated through, transfer to serving dish.

A
Supper
of Beef

Texas claims chicken fried steak for itself, and that's all right. Our lower corner tie to the Longhorn State allows us to also claim it, too, and so many of our eateries do it marvelously well. The hammering of the meat, much like the sound that once woke me for breakfast, is a given with this operation. Sure, you can purchase your meat pre-beaten, but why not use this as an excellent opportunity to get out your frustrations?

Chicken fried steak is one of the options I turn to when I end up with a squirrelly piece of meat - like big fat, membranous veins of fat through the heart of a roast that I couldn't see from the outside, or a chunk bisected by silverskin. **The meat mallet is the great equalizer,** which means I can trim to my heart's delight and slice what's leftover thick to go under the brutal smashing.

While a pan-crusted chicken fried steak is nothing to sneeze at, I consider those to be more of the country variety (see, there's a difference!). To properly chicken fry something, I want it more in line with the way I fry chicken, which is with a dry-wet-dry layering of flavor and texture that includes breadcrumbs. Chicken fried steak, though, needs a bit more salt; hence, the good old-fashioned pantry standby, saltine crackers.

CHICKEN FRIED STEAK

4 pounds beef chuck, cube steak or round	Oil for frying
	3 eggs
Salt and pepper	1/2 teaspoon pepper sauce
3 cups flour	2 tubes (1/2 box) saltine crackers
1 teaspoon ground garlic	1/4 cup fresh parsley
More salt and pepper	Salt and pepper again

Cut steak against the grain into palm sized portions around an inch thick. Season lightly with salt and pepper.

Place a towel on your counter, and a cutting board on the towel. Using a meat mallet, beat the hell out of each piece until it is no more than 1/2 an inch thick.

In a gallon sized ziptop bag, pour one cup of flour, garlic, and a touch of salt and pepper. Shake each steak individually in the bag and set aside. Allow to dry 20 minutes.

*If you want to get ahead on chicken fried steak for breakfast, you can stop here for overnight. Just place all the steaks into the ziptop bag you used for the flour, push out the excess air, and store in the refrigerator.

156   Now turn the page.

Heat 1.5" oil in cast iron skillet.

Beat together in a flat, shallow bowl the eggs with the pepper sauce.

In a zip top bag (it can be the same bag you first shook the steaks in), place saltine crackers. Gently crush the crackers with the mallet until the largest pieces are no more than 1/8 inch. Add the remaining flour, parsley, and a bit more salt and pepper.

Individually, dip each steak into the egg wash, shake in cracker bag until coated, then drop into hot oil and fry two minutes each side. Drain on paper towels and let rest for at least 10 minutes.

Make gravy while you're resting the meat.

PEPPER GRAVY for CHICKEN FRIED STEAK

1 cup reserved pan drippings from chicken fried steak
1 cup flour
1/4 teaspoon salt
1 teaspoon black pepper
1-2 cups sweet milk (whole milk)

After last steak is removed, use a wire strainer to remove stray crust bits. Add flour, salt and pepper to the cracker bag and shake til incorporated. Whisk the contents of the bag into the hot oil and make a roux, stirring constantly.

When the gravy starts to tan, cut the heat and slowly whisk in milk until gravy reaches the consistency you desire. Stir in crispy bits. Serve over steaks, potatoes and/or biscuits.

SPICY FRIED PICKLETTES

1 jar dill pickle spears
1 cup rice flour
1 cup all purpose flour
1 teaspoon fresh dill, finely chopped
1/2 teaspoon red pepper flakes
Oil for frying
Dip of choice (optional)

Place flours, dill and red pepper flakes in gallon sized ziptop bag. Shake to incorporate.

Drain pickles (you can reserve pickle juice for drinking or fried chicken, if you like). Carefully slice each pickle LENGTHWISE into thirds.

Toss a few at a time into flour bag and shake. Set aside on plate.

Heat oil to high. Drop pieces individually into oil. Fry on high until pickles lightly brown. Remove to drain on paper towels. Serve with dip of choice.

You'll notice these pickles have no egg in the batter. The original, finalized fried pickle recipe created by Bernell Austin at the Duchess Drive-In in Atkins is a dry mix, not a batter like most other pickle recipes. It seems less likely to fall off the pickle!

The pickle is salty enough - only add salt if you like to pucker..

159

FRIED OKRA

1 pound fresh okra, sliced	3/4 cup fine-ground cornmeal
1/2 teaspoon salt	1/4 cup all-purpose flour
1/4 teaspoon black pepper	1/2 cup buttermilk
1/4 teaspoon paprika (optional)	Oil for frying

Rinse and drain okra, then cut the tips and tops off and slice crosswise into 1/3" rounds. Place in ziptop bag and pour in buttermilk.

Mix together all dry ingredients in a second ziptop bag.

Heat 1/2 inch (or more if you're frying other things) cooking oil in skillet over medium high heat.

In small handfuls, dump okra into dry ingredients bag and shake. Remove with mesh or slotted spoon, shaking off excess dry mix. Drop into hot oil and make sure pieces stay separated. Fry til golden brown, then remove to paper towel draped plate with slotted spoon. Repeat until all okra is used. Serve hot.

If serving as part of a fried catfish meal, cook after hush puppies and after pulling oil for making cream gravy.

LIGHT FRIED OKRA

1 pound okra, sliced into 1/2" pieces
1/4 cup fine cornmeal or rice flour
1 teaspoon salt
1/2 teaspoon white pepper
1 Tablespoon olive oil

Place everything but the olive oil in a ziptop bag and shake until the okra is lightly coated.

Heat olive oil in saute pan or light skillet to medium high. Pour in okra and stir often. If your skillet is light enough, toss and flip your okra frequently. Once okra begins to caramelize at the edges, immediately slip from pan to serving dish. Serve hot.

You may notice that a lot of the recipes in this book are meant for the Crock Pot. It's not a commercial endorsement of any sort of brand of slow cooking pot, but a response to our busy, always-in-motion world. When I am traveling, or busy putting a book together, it's a way to get a good, hearty meal together without a lot of concentration on the oven.

That being said, just about every Crock Pot recipe here can be replicated with a heavy-bottom stockpot on a back burner left to simmer. Feel free to make whatever adjustments you like. This sort of cooking isn't a science like bread baking; it's more art with a dib of this and a dab of that.

Thus we come to the pot roast, a dish the Crock Pot was made for. A good chunk of chuck roast, with marbled fat but cleared of any silver-skin, is optimal for this operation. Onions are essential, as are potatoes and a goodly amount of patience. The two photos here were taken four hours apart - the one on the left is a five hour roast, while the one on the right is a nine hour roast. Both are great. The one on the right is nearly butter-soft.

POT ROAST

3-4 pound chuck roast
1 pound potatoes
1 pound onions
1/3 pound carrots
1/3 pound celery
1 Tablespoon garlic powder
1 Tablespoon black pepper
1 Tablespoon salt
2 cups beef broth
1 cup red wine or 1 can blonde beer
1 Teaspoon vinegar of choice

Cut chuck roast into four pieces, trimming any hard material or silverskin but leaving some fat. Sear each piece on all sides in dry skillet, then place in Crock Pot.

Cut carrots, celery and onions into 1-2" pieces - they will have a long time to simmer, and larger pieces take longer to cook through. Cut potatoes into inch thick chunks, unless using fingerling potatoes.

Place vegetables in pot with all other ingredients. Set on high. After an hour, turn to low and allow to cook through at least four hours. Season to taste with salt, pepper, pepper sauce or your choice of flavors. Serve by itself or over bread of choice.

If you like a thicker broth, make a roux of 1/2 cup butter to 1/2 cup flour. Get it to just past tan, then remove from heat and stir into pot. Or make up the brown gravy recipe in this book and pour it in.

Kat Robinson

Research on Mongolia doesn't result in the seasonings found in this recipe. No, the Mongolian flavor found here is that found in many popular Chinese restaurants, what has become to Americans "Mongolian flavor." That's all right - this is still a very tender, delectable selection, which utilizes cheap cuts of beef. There are a lot of possible substitutions here, and if you wish you can also add more heat by using Chinese chili peppers or a dash of Sriracha.

MONGOLIAN-STYLE ROASTED BEEF

2 pounds beef stew meat or chuck roast, cubed
   or any similar cuts - round, short rib or even sirloin tip
1 cup beef broth
1 package onion soup mix
   or 1 cup onions + 1 Tablespoon butter +1 teaspoon salt
1/2 cup dark soy sauce
   or 3/4 cup regular soy sauce
3 garlic cloves, shaved fine
2 inches of a fresh hand of ginger
1 bunch or 1 cup chopped green onions
1 Tablespoon red pepper flakes
3 Tablespoons all-purpose flour
   or 1 Tablespoon cornstarch
   dissolved in 1/2 cup water
Sesame seeds for garnish (optional)

Set Crock Pot to high heat. In a saucepan, saute onions in butter and salt if not using onion soup mix.

Add to saucepan beef broth, onion soup mix (if not using sautéed onions) and half of the soy sauce until reduced by 1/3. Move to Crock Pot.

Add beef in pieces no larger than 1" in size to Crock Pot and coat thoroughly with onion reduction. Add remainder of soy sauce, garlic, ginger, green onion and red pepper flakes along with two cups water. Stir.

Place lid and continue to heat on high for 2 hours. Do not stir more than once a half hour.

After the initial 2 hours in the Crock Pot, add the slurry of flour or cornstarch and incorporate completely. Replace lid and allow to cook for at least one hour more.

Serve over rice and garnish with sesame seeds, if desired.

Steaks don't usually end up in cookbooks, at least not like this. There's an assumption that everyone knows how to cook a steak.

Well, I like my steaks medium rare, because I like the flavor of the beef. I also like to bring dinner to the table in easy to eat portions - since, frankly, much of our in-house dining here is lap-borne plates or on TV trays. There's a lot of working through meals here, not just with me but Grav with his woodcut block production and Hunter with her schoolwork. With the pandemic, the three of us are all working from home. Perhaps I should be a better example and set the table for each meal, but honestly, there hasn't been as much time as I would have suspected I'd have.

That being said, there's an easy process to properly season steak, and it requires just a little patience. And if you like them cooked like I do, they'll be as tender as the soft part of your hand between your forefinger and thumb, just like Anthony Michael of the Cross Eyed Pig BBQ Company once showed me.

STEAK FOR DINNER

4 steaks of choice - we like sirloin or ribeye, 1" to 2" thick
2 Tablespoons Worcestershire sauce
1-2 Tablespoons Cavender's Greek Seasoning
    or Cotham's Hamburger Seasoning
1 teaspoon coarse ground black pepper
2 teaspoons coarse grain salt

Mix seasoning blend, Worcestershire sauce and black pepper in a ziptop bag. Drop in steaks and massage the blend into the meat. Let rest 15-20 minutes in the fridge.

Put a nice, thick-bottomed skillet on the stove - cast iron or steel-clad will work fine, non-stick aluminum will do in a pinch. Heat it on the highest flame, until a little water dropped into the pan dances and pops. Scatter salt on the surface.

Take each steak and carefully place it directly on the surface of the pan, making sure there's room for all four steaks without overlap. Now leave it alone on the heat - two minutes for rare, three and half for medium rare, or five for medium. Pick up each steak with tongs and repeat the procedure for the other side. After the amount of time for the rareness you desire, pull each steak out with tongs and allow to rest on a cutting board or plate. Leave steaks alone for 10 minutes.

Slice on the diagonal, against the grain. Taste your steak before you add salt or sauce. It's nice as it is. Don't ruin it like a heathen.

167

I was an adult before I realized that folks outside of Arkansas don't seem to have the same sort of reverence we do for gravy, particularly brown gravy. I just assumed that gravy was a condiment anywhere you went. Visits to the northeast and Florida cured me of that assumption.

The idea of said gravy on rice was even more profound. I mean, I have eaten this combination all my life, from childhood on. Brown gravy requires no meat, can be made from only shelf stable items, and goes with so many things. Want to get fancy? Throw in a can of sliced mushrooms with their juice and reduce it for mushroom gravy. Pour it on hamburger steak. Mashed potatoes are a no-brainer. Use it for just for a French dip. When you're poor, brown gravy is the sauce you turn to.

And maybe that's part of why brown gravy on rice has become so prevalent throughout Arkansas. It's a poor man's food. Rice is cheap. Potatoes are cheap. Bread is cheap. Something that works well with any white starch is bound to catch a foothold.

How do you make brown gravy? Here's the simple, core recipe.

BROWN GRAVY

2 cups water
Beef base or bullion cubes
(enough to make two cups)

1/4 cup oil
1/2 cup flour
1/2 teaspoon black pepper

Dissolve beef bullion or beef base into the water. Whisk together flour and black pepper.

Place oil into sauce pan and heat on medium. Once oil is hot, add flour mixture and keep stirring with wire whisk until the mix is blonde. Add the bouillon/water mix, until desired thickness is reached. Immediately remove from heat. If not serving immediately, whisk again before serving. Goes great on white rice, mashed potatoes, and white bread.

Mushroom variation: Add one four ounce can sliced mushrooms by draining mushroom can into bouillon mix. Fry mushrooms in the oil and remove, leaving drippings behind. Add other ingredients as directed. Chop mushrooms and add to final product.

POOR MAN'S SANDWICH

Two slices cheap white bread, lightly toasted
1/2 cup prepared brown gravy

Lay bread slices side by side. Pour gravy over. Fold one slice over the other. Eat with a fork.

Once you get to brown gravy, you have to talk about hamburger steak. As we all know, hamburger steak is not steak. It's not even a chicken fried steak. It's ground beef in the vague representation of a steak, meant to satisfy a steak lover with flavor even if texture isn't quire what we want. It differs from Salisbury steak, which has filler material in its heart, and from traditional burgers because of what it does include.

There are two ways to prepare hamburger steak, and they both involve gravy. A beef patty in this fashion without gravy is just a weird burger.

HAMBURGER STEAK

1 pound ground beef
1 Tablespoon Worcestershire sauce
2 Tablespoons dried onion
1 teaspoon garlic powder
1/2 teaspoon salt
1/4 teaspoon pepper
1/4 teaspoon paprika (optional)
1/4 teaspoon dry mustard (optional)
1 recipe brown gravy or mushroom gravy (previous page)
1 small onion, sliced into ringlets (second version)
Oil for frying

Mix together Worcestershire sauce and dry ingredients. Work into ground beef. Form into four to six patties. Place on plate in refrigerator for 20 minutes (you can make your gravy at this time).

Heat oil to high in skillet. Remove hamburger steaks from fridge and immediately lay into the pan.

Version 1: Reduce heat to medium and fry the hamburger steaks four to five minutes on each side. Remove from heat, drain. Serve under a blanket of gravy atop rice, mashed potatoes or bread.

Version 2: Heat oven to 350. Sear hamburger steaks on both sides. Remove from pan. Drop onion ringlets into the hot drippings and fry til translucent. Place steak patties in casserole, top with onions and pour gravy over all of it. Bake for 40 minutes. Serve over white starch such as rice, potatoes or bread.

Variation 3: Add mushrooms - drain one 4 ounce can of mushrooms and dice fine. Add to ground beef before incorporating other ingredients. Continue as directed. This results in a moister steak. Because mushrooms are awesome..

171

Sweet potatoes are cheap, tasty and filling. They're also a big part of winter holiday celebrations. This is a tried and true casserole served in my family that isn't topped with the marshmallow goo associated with other sweet casseroles. It also makes good use of our native pecans.

SWEET POTATO CASSEROLE

2 pounds sweet potatoes	2 eggs, well beaten
1 stick butter	1/2 cup half and half
plus 1/2 stick butter	or heavy cream
1 Tablespoon vanilla	1/2 teaspoon salt
1/4 cup brown sugar	1 teaspoon cinnamon
plus 2 Tablespoons brown sugar	1/2 cup pecan halves

Boil sweet potatoes. When soft, remove from pot and let dry..

Melt 1/2 stick of butter. Stir in 2 Tablespoons brown sugar and the cinnamon. Toss pecan halves, completely coating. Set aside.

Heat oven to 350 degrees. Pull skins off sweet potatoes and mash.

Melt stick of butter and mix in vanilla, remaining brown sugar, and salt. Beat eggs and heavy cream together. Pour both mixtures in to the sweet potatoes and fold together. Turn out into a greased 13x9 casserole and top with sugared pecans.

Bake until set in the center, 30-35 minutes.

I have easily eaten my weight in yellow squash in my lifetime. We saute it, we make it into casseroles, I've even had it in a pie before. Because it's so easy to grow here, it's everywhere. And that's okay - you can't go wrong with a mess of squash as a side to whatever you want to cook. It also doesn't need a lot of batter to crisp it up as a fried dish. It caramelizes better without a bulky double dip, and it comes out slightly sweet.

FRIED YELLOW SQUASH

2 yellow squash
1 cup flour
1 cup oil (for frying)
1 teaspoon salt
1 teaspoon pepper
1/4 cup milk
1 egg

Slice squash into 1/4 inch thick rounds. Heat oil in skillet over medium heat. Sift together flour, salt and pepper. Beat egg together with milk. Dip all rounds into flour mixture, then dip in egg mixture and dip back into flour. Fry in single layer in skillet until brown on both sides. Dry on paper towels. Serve hot.

174

I was a Girl Scout, and my daughter is one now as well. It's a lot different now. When I was in a troop in the 1980s, we camped a lot, a couple to each tent on cots with our sleeping bags. We woke up each day to a camp alert, participated in flag ceremony, ate breakfast and went about our days learning how to mark our trails through the woods with broken sticks and rocks stacked on top of each other. We learned knots and archery and how to construct basic campsites and fire circles. And we learned how to cook over those fires.

These days, Girl Scouts focuses on leadership and STEM studies, but still has a whole track of outdoor badges and activities to pursue. Hunter sells cookies to go to camp each year. I'm teaching her some of the dishes I learned how to make at camp - which includes what you can make with an old fashioned mess kit, aluminum foil and ingenuity. These sweet potatoes are one of the tastiest.

FOIL WRAPPED SWEET POTATO PACKET

1 sweet potato	1 teaspoon brown sugar
1/4 cup pecans	1 teaspoon butter

Slice sweet potato lengthwise. Lay out a piece of foil. Place butter, pecans and brown sugar in center. Place half of sweet potato on either side. Drugstore fold the foil around the ingredients, making sure to fold over the top. Place in the campfire coals with tongs or shovel, or bake in 350 degree oven, for 40 minutes. Retrieve foil packet, open and serve.

TIN FOIL APPLE

1 large apple
1 Tablespoon Red Hots
   or 1 teaspoon chopped pecans, 1 teaspoon brown sugar, 1 pat butter
   or 2 large marshmallows
   or 1 teaspoon cinnamon, 1/4 teaspoon nutmeg, 1 pat butter
   or 1 Tablespoon peanut butter, 1 pat of butter, 1 teaspoon honey

Cut through top of apple with corer and remove 3/4 of the core, leaving the bottom. Pack selection of ingredients into apple. Drugstore fold the apple into a packet. Place directly into coals. Remove 20 minutes later and enjoy.

How to drugstore fold: Take a two foot length of aluminum foil off the roller. Fold it in half. Place food in the center. Bend each side on a straight line to pull double layer of foil up and over. Bring two sides together at top, fold and crimp down. Fold each end over twice. To open, unfold the very center of the top seam of the foil pouch to ate its own serving dish.

Sweeter Things

I loved chocolate pan-fried pies as a kid. They weren't much, just a combination of cocoa powder. sugar and butter placed in a thinly rolled out piece of pie crust, fried in a skillet. But I didn't encounter them at a restaurant until 1997, when I noticed some behind the counter at Batten's Bakery in Paragould. Of course I grabbed one! To this day, only Batten's and the couple of Snappy's Quick Marts in Damascus and Bee Branch carry them. Frying them in butter isn't optimal, so I've developed a baked version.

OLD FASHIONED CHOCOLATE HAND PIES

2 cups sugar
1/2 cup cocoa powder

1/2 cup (one stick) butter
2 prepared pie crust doughs

Heat oven to 350 degrees. In a skillet or saucepot, combine sugar, cocoa powder and butter over low heat until incorporated into a paste. Roll out pie dough thin. Use a biscuit cutter or a tuna can cleaned with the bottom cut out to cut hand pie doughs. Place a tablespoon of filling in each one. Crimp the edges with a fork. Place on a baking sheet and bake 20 minutes or until dough is golden. Serve hot with ice cold milk, or save for later.

MAPLE SWEET POTATO HAND PIES

1.5 pounds of sweet potato
2 tablespoons real maple syrup
1/2 teaspoon vanilla

1/2 teaspoon cinnamon
1/4 teaspoon salt
2 balls pie crust dough

Boil or bake sweet potatoes. Remove skin. Mash (not puree) together with syrup, vanilla, cinnamon and salt.

Roll both pie dough balls flat into circles. Cut in half. Arrange 1/4 filling on one side with one inch dough left around side. Fold over and crimp with a fork. Bale at 350 degrees for 35-40 minutes. Serve hot or cold.

My eight years producing the morning show for Today's THV, the CBS affiliate here in Little Rock, were formative for the relationships built there and the knowledge absorbed. I had an incredible crew that stayed together throughout that time, and three of the very best anchors in the business.

Every Thanksgiving, we put on a marvelous and relaxed show and then sat down together for a dinner for breakfast, where we would enjoy each other's company. The build-up to Christmas saw is bringing all sorts of dishes to share.

One of my more popular dishes was banana nut bread. I would save bananas throughout the year - they'd start to get a little spotty and I'd put them in the freezer, to have the on-hand for the epic ,baking that would take place in the last month and a half of each year. Bananas were common on our crew... to the point that B..J. Sams and I more than once had conversations about floam, the stringy part between the flesh of a banana and its peel. B.J., for the record, was very anti-floam.

I had a fellow cooking aficionado on my crew. Throughout the year, Bill Ritter and I would occasionally bring dishes for each other to try. Bill came out and even worked in a few of my kitchens at SCA events. I think he may have been just as disappointed as I was when I was disqualified from Next Food Network Star in 2007, just because I had a job title of producer, even though that wasn't a cable TV show producing position. For the record, Guy Fieri won that season, giving rise to the running joke that Fieri stole my life.

I don't make banana nut bread or banana bread much now, since Grav has a banana allergy. But sometimes I find the need and the desire to create a batch.

BANANA BREAD or BANANA NUT BREAD

3-4 overripe bananas	2 1/4 cups all-purpose flour
1/2 pound (2 sticks) butter at room temperature	1 teaspoon baking soda
	1 teaspoon cinnamon
1 1/2 cups sugar	1 teaspoon salt
3 eggs	1/2 cup chopped pecans
1 teaspoon vanilla extract	or walnuts (optional)
6 ounces sour cream or buttermilk	1 cup brown sugar
	Cooking spray or additional butter

Preheat oven to 350 degrees. Grease two 9"x5"pans or one Bundt pan.

Blend butter and sugar together until fluffy. Incorporate all other wet ingredients. Sift together flour, cinnamon, baking soda and salt. Add wet ingredients and fold together. Fold in nuts if you're using them. Pat brown sugar onto sides of pan. Pour in batter. Cook for 55 minutes (loaf pans)/65 minutes (Bundt pan) until knife comes out clean.

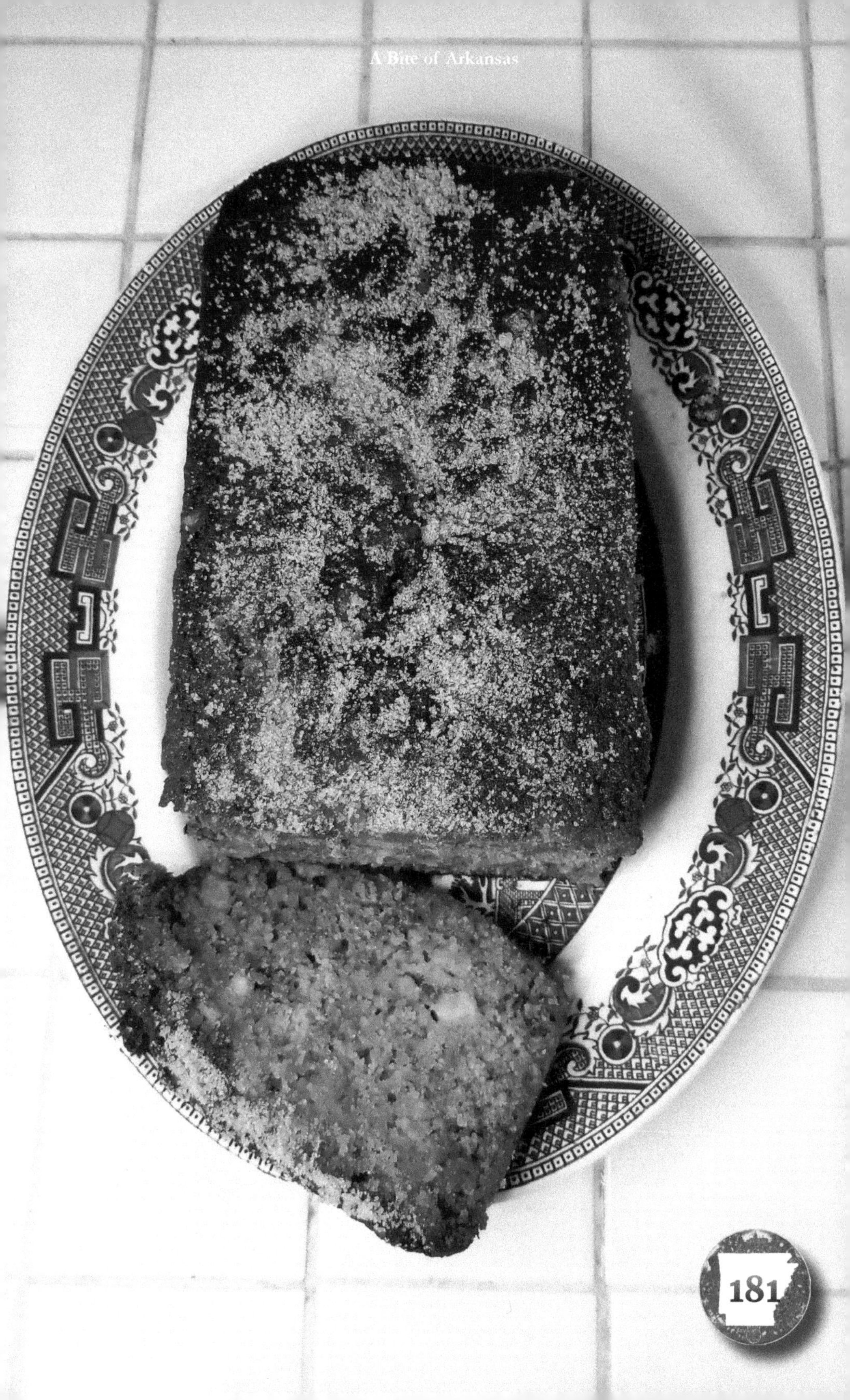

Kat Robinson

The summer plate is an Arkansas tradition that is overlooked by our peers in the culinary world, but which deserves an explanation and joy unto itself. It bears as little tie to exact description as "a picnic" or "a buffet," being based more on its enaction than its contents. The short description is a cold meal served at midday during the summer months, featuring fresh local fruits and vegetables. But it can be many more things - which is why both the plate on the left and the plate on the right qualify.

There's no set tradition recorded for posterity (unless you count my references in previous books or the few articles that have born their own fruit over the past several years). Ask any Arkansawyer whose past includes rural life, and they'll nod and share their favored items. The idea behind the dish appears to date back to our pre-air-conditioned days, when it was verboten in many homes to turn on the stove and thus head up

The first time I tried a curried dish in an Indian restaurant, I cried.
It was 1995. My boyfriend took me to Star of India and insisted I try the vindaloo, since that's what Dave Lister loved so much on *Red Dwarf.* I wasn't prepared for the rather hot, bold spicing and broke into tears. Bless his heart, Sami Lal came over and asked what was wrong and asked me if I'd like to try something different. A few minutes later, he returned to our table with a mild chicken tikka korma. I was apprehensive, but on first bite I realized I'd found something really really marvelous.

I started studying different sorts of Indian and Pakistani food shortly thereafter. Learning about regional and historical cuisine led me to start experimenting with my own curries and the spices that went into them. I learned that the whole idea of curry powder came from the English, specially designed to replicate flavors of India once countrymen who had been stationed on the subcontinent returned to their home in the British Isles. I learned how to cook directly from toasting spices on up.

Making curry this way takes a lot of time and patience. So... I also make curry powder with toasted, dehydrated and ground spices, to suit my own tastes. You may not have the time to go through the efforts of toasting and crushing your own spices. If you do, contact me and we'll talk curry. If you're really really just wanting some tasty eats now, here's a quick curry you can whip together in your own kitchen.

KAT'S QUICK CURRY

1 pound chicken, cubed
(dark meat is better)
8 ounces yogurt
2 Tablespoons turmeric, halved
2 Tablespoons cumin, halved
1 Tablespoon ground garam masala
1/2 teaspoon salt
1-2 teaspoons chili sauce (optional)

1/4 teaspoon ground coriander
1/4 teaspoon pepper
2 Tablespoons ghee or butter
1/2 cup half and half
or coconut milk
3 Tablespoons honey (optional)

Place chicken, yogurt, a tablespoon turmeric and a tablespoon cumin into a gallon sized ziptop bag. Massage yogurt and spices into the chicken. Place in refrigerator for two hours before cooking. Drain and let sit in colander five minutes before cooking.

Mix together remaining turmeric and cumin along with other dry spices. Toss chicken in spices. Heat ghee in skillet. Drop chicken into hot ghee and stir fry, making sure to heat all sides of chicken. Add half and half or coconut milk, along with honey if you want it sweet or chili sauce if you want it hot (or both). Stir and cover, reducing heat to medium low (curry should slightly bubble). Allow to cook chicken through and sauce to thicken. When chicken is done, serve with its sauce over rice or with naan.

Two things we have tons of here in Arkansas - zucchini in the summer and apples in the fall. There are folks who will force either upon you in the workplace, and a bevy that come to farmers markets statewide. What's to be done? Make sweet bread, of course.

During self-isolation, my daughter developed an affinity for zucchini bread, asking for it and consuming whole batches in a span of days or even hours at time.

ZUCCHINI BREAD

3 cups flour
1/4 teaspoon baking powder
1 teaspoon baking soda
1 teaspoon salt
3 eggs
1 cup oil

2 1/2 cups sugar
1 teaspoon vanilla extract
1 teaspoon cinnamon
2 cups diced zucchini
1 cup chopped pecans

Heat oven to 350 degrees.

Sift flour, baking powder, baking soda and salt together. Combine eggs, oil, sugar, vanilla, and cinnamon in mixer bowl; mix well. Add dry ingredients; mix well. Stir in zucchini and pecans.

Spoon into two greased loaf pans or muffin tins with 24 cups total. Bake at 350 degrees for one hour. Remove to wire rack to cool.

APPLE BREAD

1 cup butter at room temperature
2 cups sugar
4 eggs
4 cups all-purpose flour
2 teaspoons baking soda
2 teaspoons cinnamon

1 teaspoons salt
1/4 teaspoon cloves
4 cups apples, diced
1/4 cup chopped pecans or walnuts (optional)

Heat oven to 350 degrees. Grease two loaf pans or 24 muffin tin cups.

Combine flour, baking soda, cinnamon, cloves and salt. Cream butter and sugar together. Beat eggs and add to creamed butter. Fold wet ingredients into dry ingredients. Fold apples into batter. Spoon mixture into greased pan.

Place in the oven for 50-60 minutes, until inserted knife comes out clean. Remove from oven and invert on wire rack. Allow to cool 15 minutes before serving. Cover any leftovers.

As you can see, I love fruit and vegetable breads. They're great for making in advance and taking places. This particular treat is quite tart, making it perfect for brunch or tea.

LEMON BLUEBERRY BREAD

4 Tablespoons butter	1/2 teaspoon salt
3/4 cups sugar	3/4 cup milk
2 eggs, slightly beaten	1 cup fresh blueberries
2 teaspoons grated lemon rind	
2 cups flour	2 Tablespoons lemon juice
2 1/2 teaspoons baking powder	2 Tablespoons sugar

Preheat oven to 350 degrees. Grease a loaf pan.

Cream butter and sugar together. Fold in eggs and lemon rind.

Combine flour, baking powder and salt. Add to butter and egg mixture, alternating with milk. beating until smooth after each addition. Fold in blueberries.

Pour batter into pan and place in oven, baking at 350 degrees for 55-60 minutes or until inserted knife comes out clean.

Remove pan from oven and place on rack for 10 minutes. Combine reserved sugar and lemon juice and pour over loaf.

If you prefer a bread that's not so sweet, this carrot bread could be just what you're looking for. It's sweet enough to enjoy with just a little butter for breakfast, or slightly toasted as a side bread during brunch. It's also a good way to get your kids to eat carrots if they're generally opposed to the idea.

CARROT BREAD

2 eggs	1 teaspoon cinnamon
1 cup sugar	1/2 teaspoon nutmeg
2/3 cup oil	1/2 teaspoon salt
1 1/2 cups all-purpose flour	1 1/2 cups finely shredded carrots
3/4 teaspoon baking soda	1/2 cup chopped walnuts (optional)

Heat oven to 350 degrees. Grease a 9x5" loaf pan.

Beat eggs, then add sugar and oil and blend thoroughly. Combine dry ingredients and fold into egg mixture. Mix well.

Fold in carrots and walnuts. Lay into pan and bake for about an hour. Cool in pan for 10 minutes, then invert on wire rack to cool. Keep in sealed container..

BASIC DESSERT BREAD PUDDING RECIPE

4 cups bread of any sort   2 cups milk
4 eggs   1/2 cup sugar

Beat together eggs and milk. Add sugar if making a sweet pudding. Fold in bread. Spread in 9x13 or similar pan. Bake at 350 degrees for 45-50 minutes or until knife comes out clean.

Apple Cinnamon bread pudding: Add 1 Tablespoon cinnamon, 1/2 teaspoon nutmeg and 1/4 teaspoon cloves to egg and milk mixture. Fold 1 cup sliced apples into mix after bread is added.

New Orleans style bread pudding: Add 1/2 cup golden raisins. After baking, serve with a sauce of 1/2 cup butter melted with 1 cup rum or whiskey.

Pineapple upside down bread pudding: Add contents of 1 can crushed pineapple and fold in 1/2 cup maraschino cherries.

Chocolate bread pudding: After all items are mixed, fold in 1/2 cup semi-sweet chocolate chips and 1/2 cup white chocolate chips. After baking, melt 1/2 cup milk chocolate chips and drizzle over top.

Blueberry white chocolate bread pudding: Fold in 8 ounces frozen blueberries and 1 cup white chocolate chips. Can be topped with melted white chocolate.

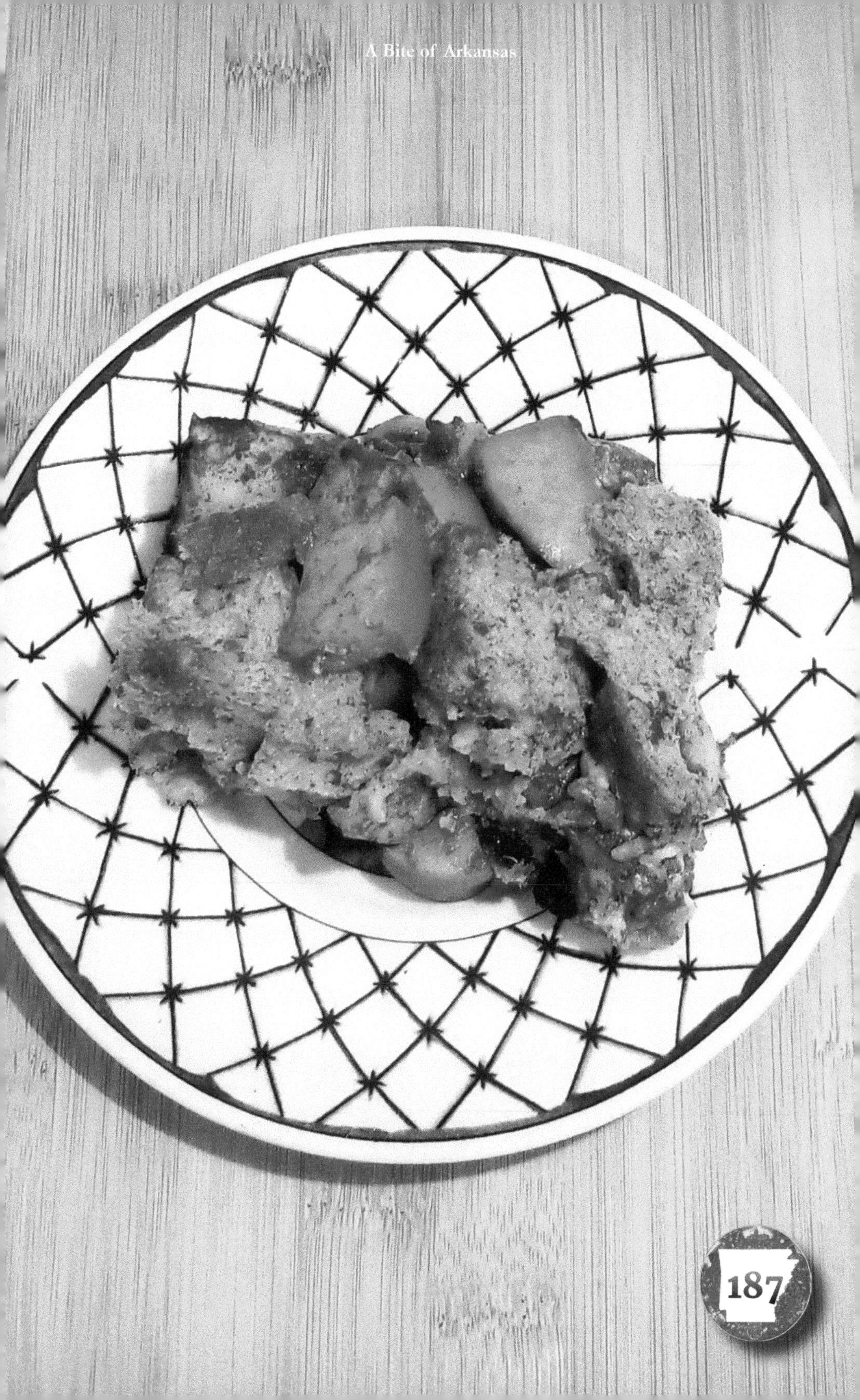

We have a real love affair with strawberries here. The first of the crop appears at the end of April, with the bulk of harvest in May and early June. Flats of juicy berries are brought home for snacking, baking and putting up. It's almost a responsibility to ensure you have ready-to-enjoy strawberries throughout the year, often contained in a reused Cool Whip Container. To wit:

STRAWBERRIES FOR FREEZING

1 quart fresh strawberries
1/2 cup confectioner's sugar

Remove caps and slice strawberries. Lay into plastic storage containers in layers, alternating with scattered teaspoon-fulls of confectioner's sugar. Fill containers to top but don't press berries down - they'll shrink a bit over time. Place in freezer. To use, pull out a container and let thaw in the fridge before using. Makes own syrup!

Once you have your strawberries put up, gotta shortcake that mess,. Or, tall cake it. While the traditional go-to around here has long been cuppa cake (a cup of butter, a cup of sugar, a cup of flour and an egg), I like this butterless, heavy cream cake.

HEAVY CREAM YELLOW CAKE

2 cups all purpose flour
2 teaspoons baking powder
3/4 teaspoon salt
1 1/2 cups heavy cream, cold
3 large eggs, at room temperature
1 teaspoon pure vanilla extract
1 cup plus 2 tablespoons superfine sugar

Sift together flour, baking powder and sugar. Heat oven to 350 degrees.

In a mixer, whip heavy cream until it forms peaks. In separate bowl, whisk vanilla into eggs, then slowly pour into cream in mixing bowl while blending, until it's the consistency of mayonnaise. Slowly incorporate sugar. Fold in flour mixture. Bake in two 9" rounds or one 13x9" baking pan until inserted knife comes out clean.

To assemble: Cut cake horizontally. Layer with strawberries and whipped cream. Serve immediately.

Leftovers can be used to make a wonderful trifle. Just cut remaining cake into squares, fold together with whipped cream and strawberries, reserving strawberry syrup to drizzle over the top. It'll turn pink. That''s OK.

WATERMELON PRESERVES

5 cups watermelon rind	1 teaspoon salt
2 1/2 cups sugar	1 lemon

Remove skin of melon (the leathery green part). Leave 1/8 inch red part of fruit if you can. Cut into cubes no larger that 1/2 inch. Place in bowl. Slice lemon into 1/2 inch disks and fold into watermelon rind. Add salt to sugar and then cover the fruit completely. Refrigerate overnight.

Pour contents into pot and bring to medium heat. Let simmer for up to two hours, until the watermelon becomes translucent. Remove lemon. Pack hot into jars and seal by pressure cooker method.

Serve as a garnish for cookies or biscuit, or atop a dollop of cream cheese on crackers. Also works well in mixed beverages.

While you'll find pie anywhere you go in Arkansas, cobbler is also common, particularly on country buffets. In fact, it's so expected on buffets, you'll find it on Asian buffets next to almond cookies and ice cream machines. Like many, I adore cobbler, particularly when fruit is fresh and in season - and peach cobber is at the top of that list. Several times, I have judged peach cobbler at the Johnson County Peach Festival. Some cobbers are better than others, but I have yet to find a peach cobbler I didn't like.

PEACH COBBLER

4 cups all-purpose flour	2 pounds fresh peaches, sliced
1 teaspoon salt	1 cup sugar
1 cup + 2 Tablespoons butter	1 teaspoon lemon juice
5 Tablespoons ice water	1 teaspoon vanilla extract
Butter for greasing pan	1/2 teaspoon cinnamon

Heat oven to 425 degrees. Grease 13x9" pan. Combine 3 cups of flour and salt. Cut in butter until dough resembles crumbs. Add water until dough can form a ball. Halve dough and roll out. Lay one rolled dough across bottom of baking dish. Place in oven 10 minutes to bake.

In a sauce pan, melt butter. Add sugar, lemon juice, vanilla and cinnamon and incorporate. Toss peach slices in one cup flour, the fold peaches into melted butter mixture and coat. Remove from heat.

Reduce oven heat to 400 degrees. Fill bottom crust with peach mixture, then cover with remaining rolled-out dough. Cover with foil. Bake 30 minutes, remove foil, and bake 20 more minutes. Serve hot.

PEACH VANILLA CREAM PIE

6 whole graham cracker planks, pounded to crumbs
1 Tablespoon butter
1 8 ounce package cream cheese at room temperature
1/2 can sweetened condensed milk
2 teaspoons vanilla
1 Tablespoon lemon juice
4 fresh ripe peaches, sliced

Melt butter. Blend together graham cracker crumbs with butter, then press into pie pan. Set aside.

Blend together cream cheese, sweetened condensed milk, vanilla and lemon juice. Pour into pie crust. Place peach slices on top. Cover and refrigerate until ready to serve.

Variation: Melt together 1 Tablespoon butter, 1 Tablespoon brown sugar and 1 teaspoon vanilla. Fold in peach slices. Array peach mixture atop cream cheese filling. Cover and refrigerate until ready to serve.

LEMON ICEBOX PIE

1 sleeve Girl Scout Trefoil (shortbread) cookies or equivalent
3/4 stick butter, melted
2 Tablespoons sugar, halved
1/4 teaspoon salt
1 can sweetened condensed milk
1 (8 ounce package cream cheese, softened
zest from 1 lemon
1/4 cup lemon juice from same lemon
1/2 cup heavy whipping cream
1 Tablespoon sugar

Crush cookies. Place in bowl with butter, salt and a tablespoon of sugar Use a food processor to pulse cookies into fine crumbs. Place in a medium bowl. Stir in melted butter, 1 tablespoon sugar, and salt. Mix together and then press mixture into a pie pan. Refrigerate until ready to fill.

Blend together sweetened condensed milk, cream cheese, lemon zest, and lemon juice until smooth. Beat whipping cream and sugar together until peaks form. Fold into cream cheese mixture. Pour into crust and refrigerate until firm (about two hours).

FRESH PEAR TART

1 prepared pie crust
4 fresh pears (combine at least two different pear varietals)
1 stick butter
1 teaspoon vanilla
2 Tablespoons brown sugar

Blind bake crust. Let cool.

Slice pears 1/4 inch thick from top to bottom. Arrange half in pie crust with edges overlapping.

Heat oven to 350 degrees.

In a saucepan, combine butter, vanilla and brown sugar. Pour half over bottom layer of pear slices. Arrange remaining pear slices on top. Pour over other half of vanilla butter mixture.

Bake at 350 degrees for 30 minutes, until pears are tender.

FLOUR DOUGH PIE CRUST

1 1/2 sticks cold unsalted butter
3 cups all-purpose flour
1 teaspoon salt
1 tablespoon sugar
1/3 cup Crisco vegetable shortening refrigerated
1/2 cup ice water

Run butter through large-hole grater and put in the freezer. Mix salt and sugar into flour. Pull butter and shortening out of the fridge and cut it into the flour until pebble-sized crumbs are formed. Add just enough cold water to form a dough ball. Quickly wrap it in plastic and put it back in the fridge for half an hour.

Pull the dough out of the fridge and cut it in half. Roll it from center, making sure to flour the surface and the pin so the dough doesn't stick. When it's large enough, lay it across your pie pan and press in, trimming the outside edge.

Repeat with second crust, but place between wax paper sheets. Roll up and store in refrigerator until ready to use.

Or, you know, go get a refrigerated crust from the store. There's no shame in that.

I never intended to end up "the pie lady," because frankly I don't make all that many sweet pies. But with two books written on the subject of pie in Arkansas, the tag has stuck. So for my last recipe to share this time around, I present to you a perfect, lovely pie for a summer's day, filled with fresh, lovely Arkansas blueberries.

BLUEBERRY PIE

1 single layer pie crust, baked
4 ounces white chocolate chips
3/4 cup sugar
1 teaspoon unflavored gelatin
1/4 teaspoon salt

1/4 cup cold water
5 cups fresh blueberries, divided
1 Tablespoon butter
1 Tablespoon lemon juice

Heat oven to 350 degrees. Pour white chocolate chips into previously baked pie shell. Bake for 10 minutes, then remove from oven and allow to cool.

In a saucepan over medium heat, combine sugar, gelatin, salt and water until smooth. Add 3 cups blueberries. Bring to a boil; cook and stir for 2 minutes or until thickened and bubbly.

Remove from the heat. Add butter, lemon juice and remaining berries; stir until butter is melted. Cool. Pour into crust. Refrigerate.

Likewise, Etcetera

KITCHEN MEASUREMENTS

3 teaspoons = 1 tablespoon
1-1/2 teaspoons = 1/2 tablespoon
4 tablespoons = 1/4 cup
8 tablespoons = 1/2 cup
16 tablespoons = 1 cup
1 cup = 1/2 pint
2 cups = 1 pint
4 cups = 1 quart
2 pints = 1 quart
1 cup = 8 fluid ounces
32 ounces = 1 quart
2 quarts = 1/2 gallon
4 quarts = 1 gallon
1 stick of butter = 8 tablespoons = 1/2 cup

INDEX

201

Kat Robinson

Kat Robinson

My gratitude goes out to several individuals, without whom this book would not be possible.

Appreciation goes to Margie Raimondo of Urbana Farmstead and Ruth Pepler of Dogwood Hills Guest Farm for sourcing some of the produce and dairy used in this book.

Much thanks goes to my mom, Kitty Waldon, who let me take over her Little Rock kitchen and make it my own. The photographs in this book were almost entirely taken there. Mom also purchased groceries so I could dig into these culinary roots.

To Leif Hassell, who checked in on me on a daily basis through the pandemic. It was so appreciated.

I am grateful for my daughter, Hunter Robinson, who was my test subject and sounding board through the trial and photography period, for sometimes showing up in her Zooms with plates to share, and who provided continual, honest feedback.

And my appreciation goes to my partner, Grav Weldon, who was not only patient when I up and decided to relocate to write a cookbook and shoot a cooking show, but who also proofread this book. Thank you so very much.

Kat Robinson is Arkansas's food historian and most enthusiastic road warrior. The Little Rock-based author is the host of the Emmy-nominated documentary *Make Room For Pie; A Delicious Slice of The Natural State* and the Arkansas PBS show *Home Cooking with Kat and Friends*. She is a member of the Arkansas Food Hall of Fame committee, a co-chair of the Arkansas Pie Festival, and the Arkansas fellow to the National Food and Beverage Museum.

She has written nine books on food, most notably *Arkansas Food: The A to Z of Eating in The Natural State*, an alphabetic guide to the dishes, delights and food traditions that define her home state. Her two most recent travel guides, *101 Things to Eat in Arkansas Before You Die* and *102 More Things to Eat in Arkansas Before You Die* define the state's most iconic and trusted eateries. Robinson's *Another Slice of Arkansas Pie: A Guide to the Best Restaurants, Bakeries, Truck Stops and Food Trucks for Delectable Bites in The Natural State* outlines more than 400 places to find the dessert, an extraordinary accomplishment that took thousands of miles, hundreds of hours and so many bites to properly document and catalogue.

In this book, Robinson shares recipes from her own kitchen, alongside stories from her lifelong adventures in Arkansas. The book is her first state-specific cookbook. In 2020, she edited and contributed to *43 Tables: An Internet Community Cooks During Quarantine*, a collection of recipes from social media connected friends who turned to their kitchens to experiment and to feed their families during the early days of the COVID-19 pandemic response.

Her previous books include the popular *Arkansas Pie: A Delicious Slice of the Natural State* (2012), *Classic Eateries of the Ozarks and Arkansas River Valley* (2013), and *Classic Eateries of the Arkansas Delta* (2014). Robinson has also served as guest editor for the University of Arkansas publication *Arkansauce: The Journal of Arkansas Foodways*, and was recognized as the 2011 Arkansas Department of Parks and Tourism Henry Award winner for Media Support.

Her work has appeared in regional and national publications including *Food Network, Forbes Travel Guide, Serious Eats,* and *AAA Magazines,* among others. Her expertise in food research and Arkansas restaurants has been cited by *Saveur, Eater, USA Today, The Wall Street Journal, The Outline,* and the Southern Foodways Alliance's *Gravy* podcast, and her skills and talents have been celebrated in articles by *Arkansas Good Roads, Arkansas Business* and the *Arkansas Democrat-Gazette.* She has served as the keynote speaker for the South Arkansas Literary Festival and has spoken before the Arkansas Library Association and at the Six Bridges Literary Festival, Eureka Springs Books in Bloom and the Fayetteville True Lit Festival.

While she writes on food and travel subjects throughout the United States, she is best known for her ever-expanding knowledge of Arkansas food history and restaurant culture, all of which she explores on her 1200+ article website, TieDyeTravels.com. She is also the host of the podcast Kat Robinson's Arkansas.

Robinson's journeys across Arkansas have earned her the title "road warrior," "traveling pie lady," and probably some minor epithets. Few have spent as much time exploring The Natural State, or researching its cuisine. "The Girl in the Hat" has been sighted in every one of Arkansas's 75 counties, oftentimes sliding behind a menu or peeking into a kitchen.

Before entering full time into the world of food and travel writing, Kat was a television producer at Little Rock CBS affiliate THV and Jonesboro ABC affiliate KAIT, as well as a radio producer and personality for KARN Newsradio.

Kat lives with daughter Hunter and partner Grav Weldon in Little Rock.

You can contact the author at *kat@tiedyetravels.com* with questions or correspondence - or, of course, recommendations on great recipes and wonderful places to eat in Arkansas.

NOTES

CPSIA information can be obtained
at www.ICGtesting.com
Printed in the USA
LVHW071608200723
752802LV00023B/150